*"Don't judge each day by the harvest you reap
but by the seeds you plant."*

Robert Louis Stevenson

For hundreds of millions of years, plants have been implementing ingenious stratagems to make it possible for their offspring to liberate themselves and disperse. Over generations, they have perfected their design, optimized the relationship between form and function, and given birth to an enormous diversity of seeds and fruits. Encapsulated in a fleshy berry, a pod, a hull, or fitted out with ingenious appendages, seeds seize every opportunity and sometimes combine several tactics to set out on their remarkable, epic journeys.

Take a close look at their inventiveness—seeds are an endless source of wonder!

Se

Nature's Intrepid
Miracles

Cruschiform

PRESTEL
Munich · London · New York

with just a puff of air

Light and tiny, these seeds are bona fide conquistadors. The air is their ally: a simple puff is enough to carry them off to new countries they can colonize. Wearing a petticoat, a plume, or a parachute, the numerous representatives of this miniature society are full of tricks!

1. ARTICHOKE
Cynara cardunculus • x 4

You eat the base of the artichoke flower before it sets seed.

2. CLEMATIS
Clematis flammula • x 4

Its delicate plume is used as a sail as it meanders about the countryside.

3. PLANE TREE
Platanus acerifolia • x 4,5

Pranksters know that its hairy seed is an awesome itching powder.

4. ST. JOHN'S WORT
Hypericum sp. • x 43

Smaller than a grain of sand, this seed takes advantage of the slightest breeze.

5. STAR CLOVER
Trifolium stellatum • x 20

Elegant and graceful, the seed dances like a ballerina on the wind.

6. WHITE CAMPION
Silene latifolia • x 27

This feral night owl is so discreet that its dispersal often goes unnoticed.

9 with just a puff of air

Leontodon taraxacum

with just a puff of air

• DANDELION •

gone with the wind

Who hasn't blown on a dandelion and made a wish? These delicate silky spheres that dot our gardens are made up of a multitude of adventuresome seeds waiting to be spread to the four winds! Suspended from their feathery parachutes, these cheerful vagabonds rise up into the sky, seizing on favorable currents that sometimes take them kilometers away. The faithful allies of this ubiquitous plant are children who, by blowing on the seeds with full force, help them fly further and further away, messengers of their joy.

Capsella bursa-pastoris x 3

11 with just a puff of air

• SHEPHERD'S PURSE •

coins of prosperity

In former times, shepherds lived a simple life in the mountains in tune with nature. They would hang a small triangular purse, which they used as a wallet or bag for food, from their belt. Unfortunately, it was often empty... The fruits of this discreet plant have a similar shape. Although they are small and flat, they are very fertile! Each purse contains a multitude of golden-yellow coins that, sown by the wind, ensure the plant's future prosperity.

Medicago orbicularis

with just a puff of air

• BUTTON BURCLOVER •

playing hooky

Clover has been domesticated in many countries for millennia to feed livestock. Sown, cultivated, and harvested, its destiny has long been mapped out. However, when its wild side catches up with it, this forage plant likes to play hooky. When mature, its little spiral fruits detach from the plant. They roll and wander across the fields carrying their future children on the wind. At the end of the journey, the fruit disintegrates and frees its seeds to their new life.

Scabiosa x 18

13 with just a puff of air

• SCABIOUS •
little ballet pupil

As winter approaches, the scabious flower, which is widespread in the countryside, turns into an elegant ball ready to sow itself. Adorned with a ruffle and impressive petticoat, each little seed dances, held weightless in its crêpe tutu. Thus dressed, these girls of the opera house spin delicately, pirouette, jeté, and land softly... Unfortunately, the ballet is sometimes short-lived because an entire battalion of ants lie in wait on the ground to devour them.

x1 *Aristolochia elegans*

14 with just a puff of air

• BIRTHWORT •
hanging lantern

The birthwort is an extremely limber climber of the tropics. Its long stems allow it to climb up dozens of meters to find a place for itself in the sun. Its fruits, hanging like miniature lanterns, sway in the slightest breeze. Each one contains more than 300 tiny lightweight seeds awaiting the right moment to establish a new encampment. When the capsule finally opens, a host of winged seeds with a conquering spirit float out on a breath of air.

Briza maxima   x 6,5

15   with just a puff of air

• GREATER QUAKING GRASS •
the lovers' breezes

This plant, which is also known as "the grand romance" in French, secretly vibrates with love stories… Such a sentimentalist! When sunny days arrive, it stretches out its graceful stems and fragile spikelets: a fleeting affair. Subjected to the whims of the breeze, they sway and tremble with every movement of the air. Will the wind be able to free them? One fine day, the little spikes break up and each seed—nestled at the bottom of a lobe—is invited to discreetly take flight.

x10 *Papaver rhoeas*

16 with just a puff of air

• FIELD POPPY •

saltshaker of the field

A true invader is hidden behind the apparent fragility of the poppy's flowers. This pioneering species loves being the first to colonize freshly plowed areas. Raising its scarlet standards across the fields, the poppy proclaims a merciless melee to rule over the domain. When the wilted, battle-weary flower is replaced by a saltshaker-like capsule, it sprinkles a multitude of little bluish balls onto the wind: 1,000 soldiers dedicated to making the poppy empire flourish!

Digitalis purpurea x 58

17 with just a puff of air

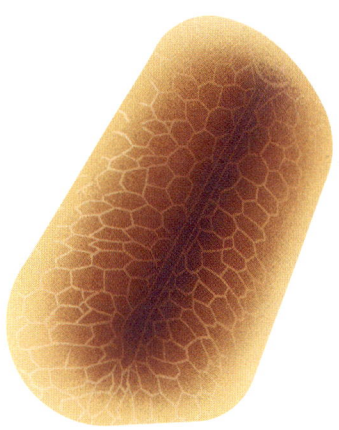

• FOXGLOVE •
the skedaddler

Foxglove seeds are extraordinarily small and light: 10,000 per gram! All it takes is a simple puff of air for them to take off, to skedaddle and spread like a cloud of dust. Due to their honeycomb structure, they have a good grip on the wind. But watch out, they don't have time to dawdle! Each seed has only a tiny reserve of food to draw on before it will finally need to germinate.

on the wind

The wind is the preferred partner of most seeds. But the biggest ones must compete in ingenuity to keep suspended or else propel themselves: wings, capes, gliders, carriages, or flying capsules…
All vehicles are permitted in this topsy-turvy airborne race!

1. AFRICAN TULIP TREE
Spathodea campanulata • x 4
The wing wrapped around the seed of this tree is as thin as tissue paper.

2. HEART PEA
Cardiospermum halicacabum • x 1,5
The fruit, inflated like a balloon, protects its 3 seeds.

3. EUROPEAN HORNBEAM
Carpinus betulus • x 4
Dressed in a cape, the hornbeam spreads easily in the forests.

4. HORA
Dipterocarpus zeylanicus • x 1,5
In the heart of Sri Lanka, this enormous tree sends its winged fruit above the forest canopy.

5. ASH
Fraxinus sp. • x 2,5
With its wind-turbine blade shape, the fruit of the ash is an acrobatics champ.

6. HOP TREE
Ptelea trifoliata • x 2
The seed, well enfolded in the waffle coat of its fruit, waits for winter to finally disperse.

7. BUSH WILLOW
Combretum • x 1
Assisted by the 4 membranous wings of its fruit, this seed has many advantages for propagating.

x 2,5

Acer saccharum

22 on the wind

• SUGAR MAPLE •

flying jewels

Standing on a bridge over a stream, a group of children armed with small vegetal propellors place their bets on a high-flying race. The wager is on the one whose airborne craft will fly the furthest. Twin maple seeds, carried by the broad wings of their fruit, have the power to stay suspended. They twirl tirelessly to slow down their intimidating dive. These aerodynamic wonders are real flying jewels, which even inspired Leonardo da Vinci in his time.

Alsomitra macrocarpa x 1,5

23 on the wind

• JAVAN CUCUMBER •
the perfect glider

With a span of 13 centimeters, this is not only one of the largest winged seed, but also the most efficient! Its membrane, as thin and transparent as tissue paper, makes it the perfect glider. It knows how to play with the rising winds, gain height, and oscillate in the air. Laid-back and light, it seems more agile than a butterfly. In 1904, Igo Etrich, the Austrian aviation pioneer, imitated its tapered shape to develop his first planes.

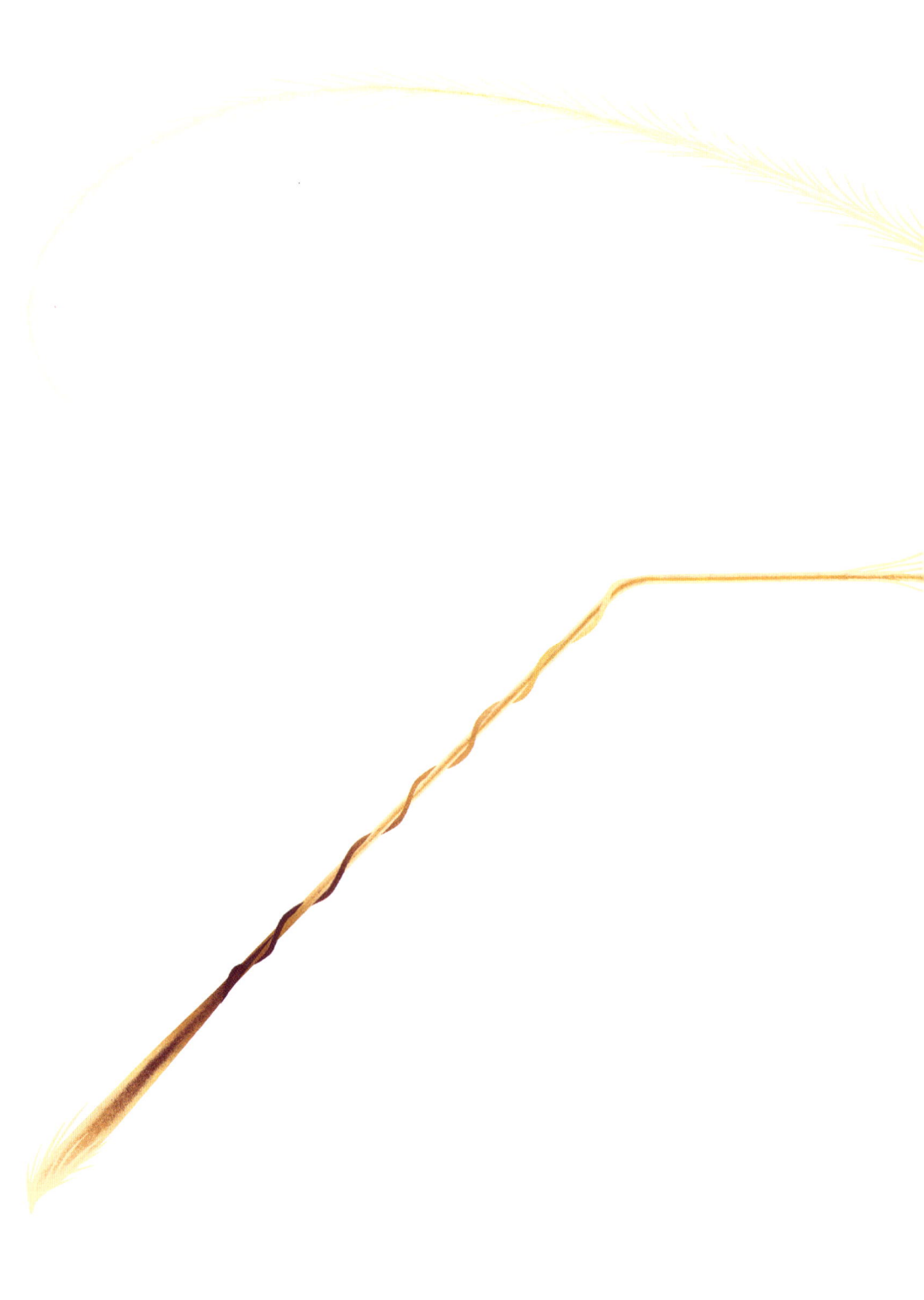

Stipa pennata — x 3

25 on the wind

• FEATHER GRASS •

golden curls

This plant, with its angelic hair, lives on the golden steppes of the Cévennes highlands in France. *Stipa pennata* is conspicuous for its long white plume with silver highlights and can measure over 20 centimeters. From dawn to dusk, it undulates and floats in the wind, scattering its seeds across the fields. It is highly sensitive to the level of humidity in the air. It straightens out in humid weather, and curls and twists when it is dry... Just the opposite of our hair!

x 1,5 *Lunaria*

on the wind

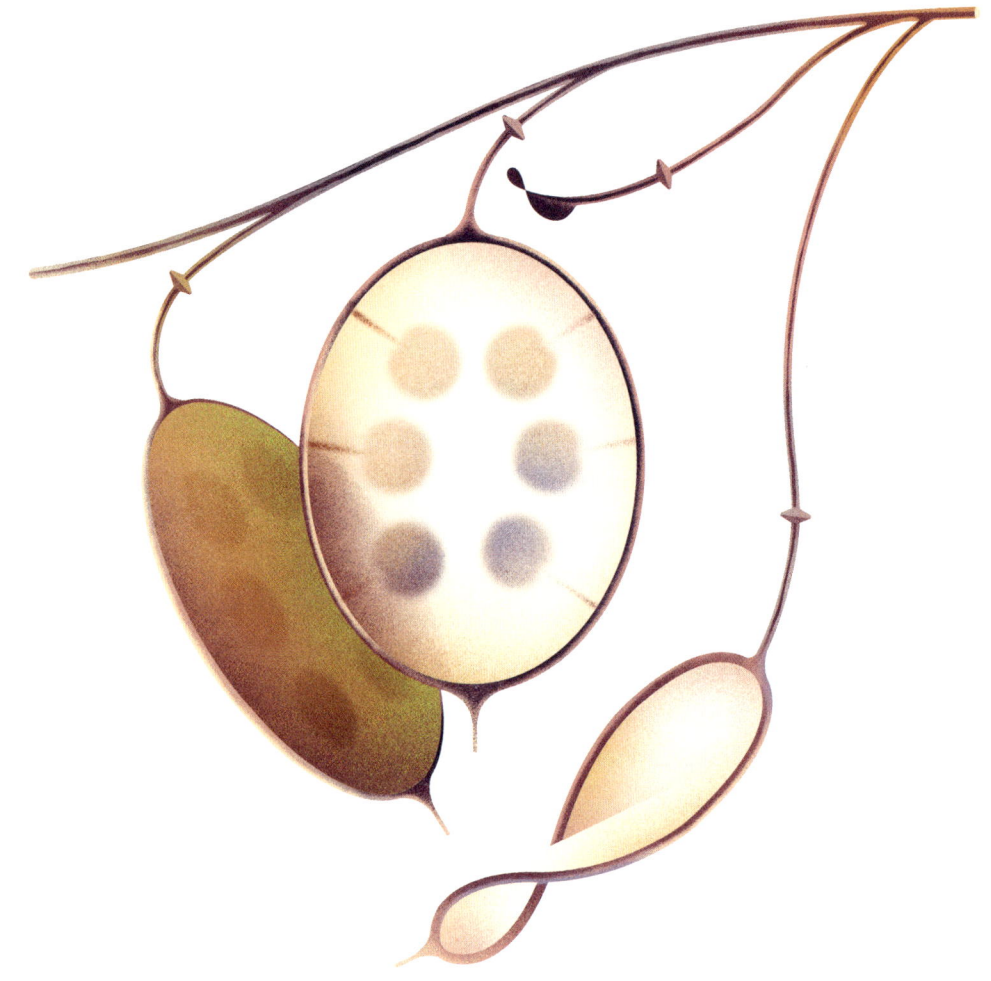

• HONESTY •
coins under the moon

Honesty, which is known as "papal money" in some countries, is round like a coin and as pearly as the moon! A familiar sight in the undergrowth, this plant is discreet when in flower and majestic when in seed. Its fruit, hardly thicker than a sheet of paper, reveals the flat seeds inside. When summer arrives, it dries up and opens in two parts leaving its putti to their destiny. The wind blows them away—but rarely more than a few meters.

Tilia x 2

27 on the wind

• LINDEN •

twirling parachutes

Who hasn't dreamed of falling asleep in the shade of a linden tree on a summer afternoon? From the beginning of July, this majestic tree is decorated with a large number of small globular fruits. These are also equipped with a long, soft green, leaf-like sail. Clinging to this vegetal parachute, the fluffy beads catch the gusts of wind and take advantage of their direction. In free flight, they twist and turn before landing daintily upon the ground.

• WILD CARROT •

a nest on the wind

Queen of wastelands and barren fields, the wild carrot outshines all tall grasses with its majestic umbel: a dome of tiny white flowers. As summer approaches, the flowers transform into so many hairy little grains, and the maternal dome curls up into a lovely, cozy nest enveloping the entire brood. When the right day comes, the offspring leave the nest on the wind in search of freedom, scattering as they go.

Colutea arborescens x 1,5

29 on the wind

• BLADDER SENNA •
the bladder tree

Popping these little pods used to be a welcome distraction for adventurers in short trousers. In summer, when the weather becomes hot on the scrub and paths near the Mediterranean, this strange fruit inflates with air. It becomes translucent and, streaked with veins, it looks like a fish bladder—hence its nickname. When it falls to the ground, it starts to roll, as light as a balloon, blown by the mistral wind ... all the way to a promised land where the seeds inside can finally germinate.

x 2 *Physalis*

30 on the wind

· JAPANESE LANTERN ·

voyage in a calyx

This little berry, which is known as "love-in-a cage" in French, grows in a calyx, a protective envelope that protects it from danger. Trapped in its gilded cage, it awaits patiently to be rescued by Prince Charming, when suddenly ... the calyx breaks loose and rolls to the ground. Aboard its carriage, it flees, carried by the wind and streaming water like a floating lantern. But the casket does not last much longer, and creatures attracted by the sweet perfume have already spotted it. Will it spread its seeds before being eaten?

Salsola tragus   x 0,5

31   on the wind

• TUMBLEWEED •
the desert tumbler

This plant is an icon of westerns. In the small desert towns that act as the setting for these great epics, it rolls across the scene as the gunfight is announced. In reality, this ball from the arid regions of North America is a terrible scourge for inhabitants. The dispersal strategy of this highly invasive plant is remarkable: when mature, it dries out, detaches from its root, and tumbles away, driven by the wind. It is a frantic race. It secretes its seeds until it reaches a watering place where it can establish itself anew!

on the water

From the runoff caused by storms to the great currents that govern our oceans, water carries certain seeds to new regions, sometimes thousands of kilometers away from their point of departure. There is only one condition for taking part in this adventure: being able to float!

1. MARY'S BEAN
Merremia discoidesperma • x 2
This seed holds the record for drifting in the ocean: ca. 28,000 kilometers.

2. WATER CALTROP
Trapa natans • x 4
Twelve whole years can pass before the seed of this fruit germinates.

3. SEA DAFFODIL
Pancratium maritimum • x 2
These black seeds, wrapped in a material like polystyrene, are very light and buoyant.

4. WHITE WATER LILY
Nymphaea alba • x 2,5
At maturity, the fruit tree's tiny seeds are equipped with a buoy to stay afloat.

5. GRAY NICKER
Caesalpinia bonduc • x 1,5
This hollow seed, which looks like a cat's eye, is able to float.

6. YELLOW WATER LILY
Nuphar lutea • x 1,5
Alas! This water fruit only spreads its seed over short distances.

7. HORSE EYE BEAN
Mucuna sloanei • x 2,5
Nearly 5,000 kilometers can separate this seed from its native soil.

35 on the water

x 0,5   *Cocos nucifera*

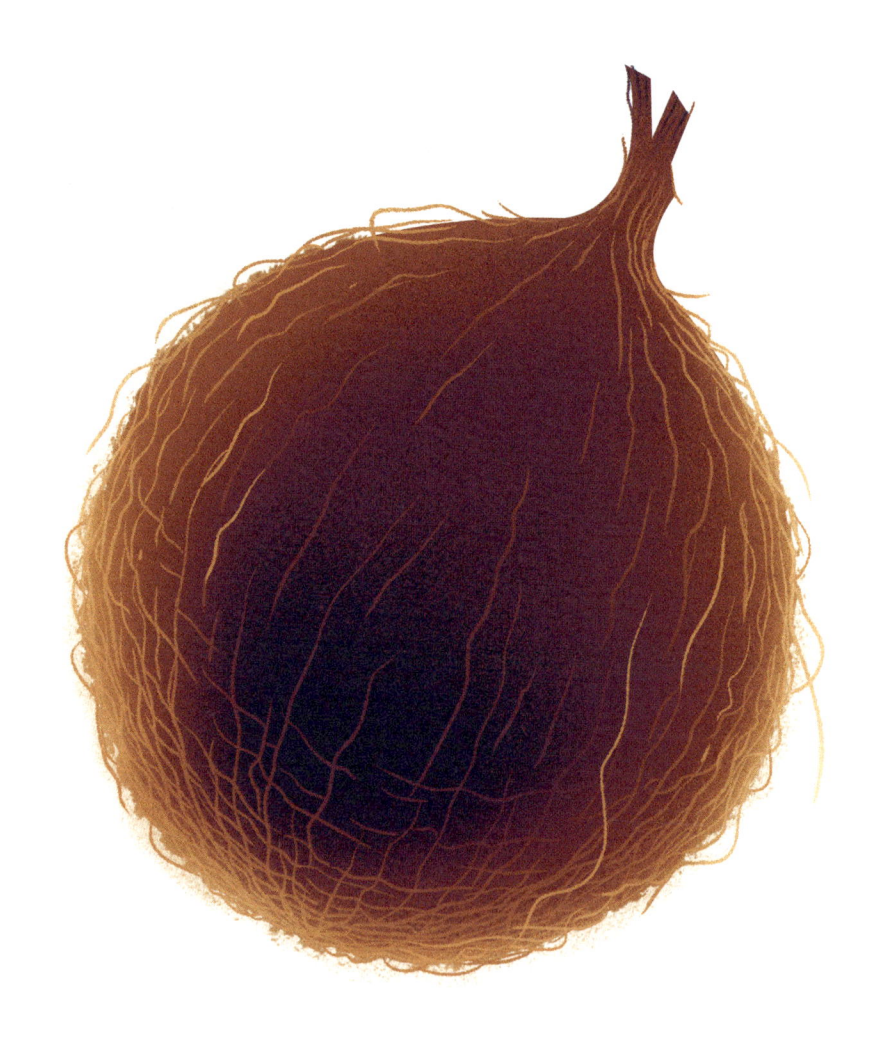

· COCONUT ·

an enigma of origins

Coconuts are among the largest seeds in the world. But that doesn't mean they can't float! Round and hollow like a balloon, they also have a thick, waterproof wadding that keeps them on the surface of water. Like a life buoy, this intrepid navigator takes to the waves. Traversing the oceans since the dawn of time, its nuts are scattered along the tropical coasts of every continent. In fact, no one knows its true origin!

Rhizophora mangle x 0,5

37 on the water

• RED MANGROVE •
family spirit

The mangrove forests on the muddy coasts of Florida have a family spirit: they form protective islands for an entire aquatic ecosystem. Their seeds, unadventurously, rarely stray from their mother's petticoats. When mature, they germinate in the same tree. An imposing tapering stem then emerges. When the time comes for them to become independent, they plunge like torpedoes into the brackish costal water and immediately root themselves at the foot of their parent.

x 1,5 　　　　　　　　　　　　　　　　　　　　　　　　　　　　　　　　　　　*Nelumbo nucifera*

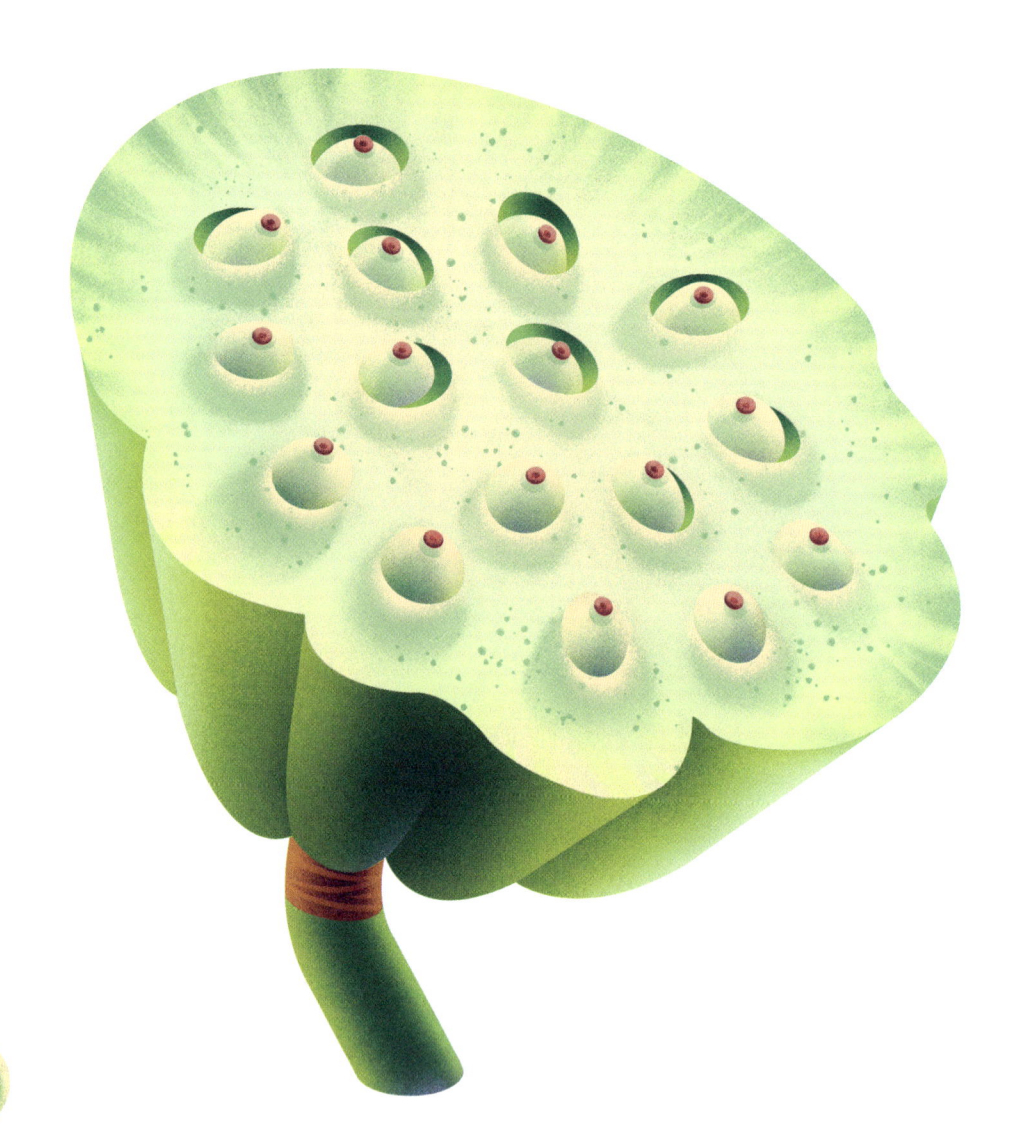

• SACRED LOTUS •
sleeping beauty

Nearly 1,300 years ago, in the northeast of the Chinese Empire, a tiny lotus seed, no bigger than an acorn, was seized by the slimy mud of the lake where it lived. The sleeping beauty in its bed of mire did not see the lake dry up or the succession of imperial dynasties. A year, three centuries, a millennium passed by before, one fine day, a handful of ingenious researchers in white coats awakened it from its long slumber to germinate, to resurrect it.

Barringtonia asiatica   x 1

39   on the water

• FISH POISON TREE •

terrible sorceress

This fruit's ability to float on the surface of the sea because of its airiness is not its biggest secret. Its nut is able to bewitch fish! Long known to the natives of New Caledonia, the toxic poison it contains was used to fish at the surface of lagoons. Crushed and diluted in the clear water, it produces a terrible brew that paralyzes the fish and brings about their slow death... This made for easy, but cruel, fishing.

x 0,5 *Entada gigas*

• SEA BEAN •

an ocean of love

Nestled in a giant pod of up to 2 meters in length, these heart-shaped seeds are long-distance champions! First transported by the rivers of Central American rainforests, they then reach the oceans, and their long journey continues. Equipped with an air pocket, they can drift for months... The currents finally take them to new lands, sometimes as far away as England, more than 20,000 kilometers from home... A record!

41 on the water

x 2 *Trapa bicornis*

on the water 42

• WATER CHESTNUT •
terrifyingly aquatic

Eerie with its ram's head shape, this inhabitant of Asia's tropical regions adapts easily to the stagnant water of the ponds it insidiously colonizes. With its formidable horns serving as arms, it clings firmly to vegetation before anchoring itself in the thick silt that will help it germinate. Not very attractive! And yet, when it is roasted over a wood fire, its delicate chestnut aroma make the mouths of little gourmands water.

Iris pseudacorus   x 1,5

43   on the water

• FLAG IRIS •

as light as a feather

This yellow iris is a plant that loves to have its feet in water. Capsules laden with golden seeds hang from its long stems waiting for the right moment to burst forth. The featherweight crew is clad in an airy, polystyrene-like material, itself covered with a thin layer of waterproof wax. With their wetsuits on, each member of this merry flotilla can sail for 12 months, against wind and tide, without fear of sinking.

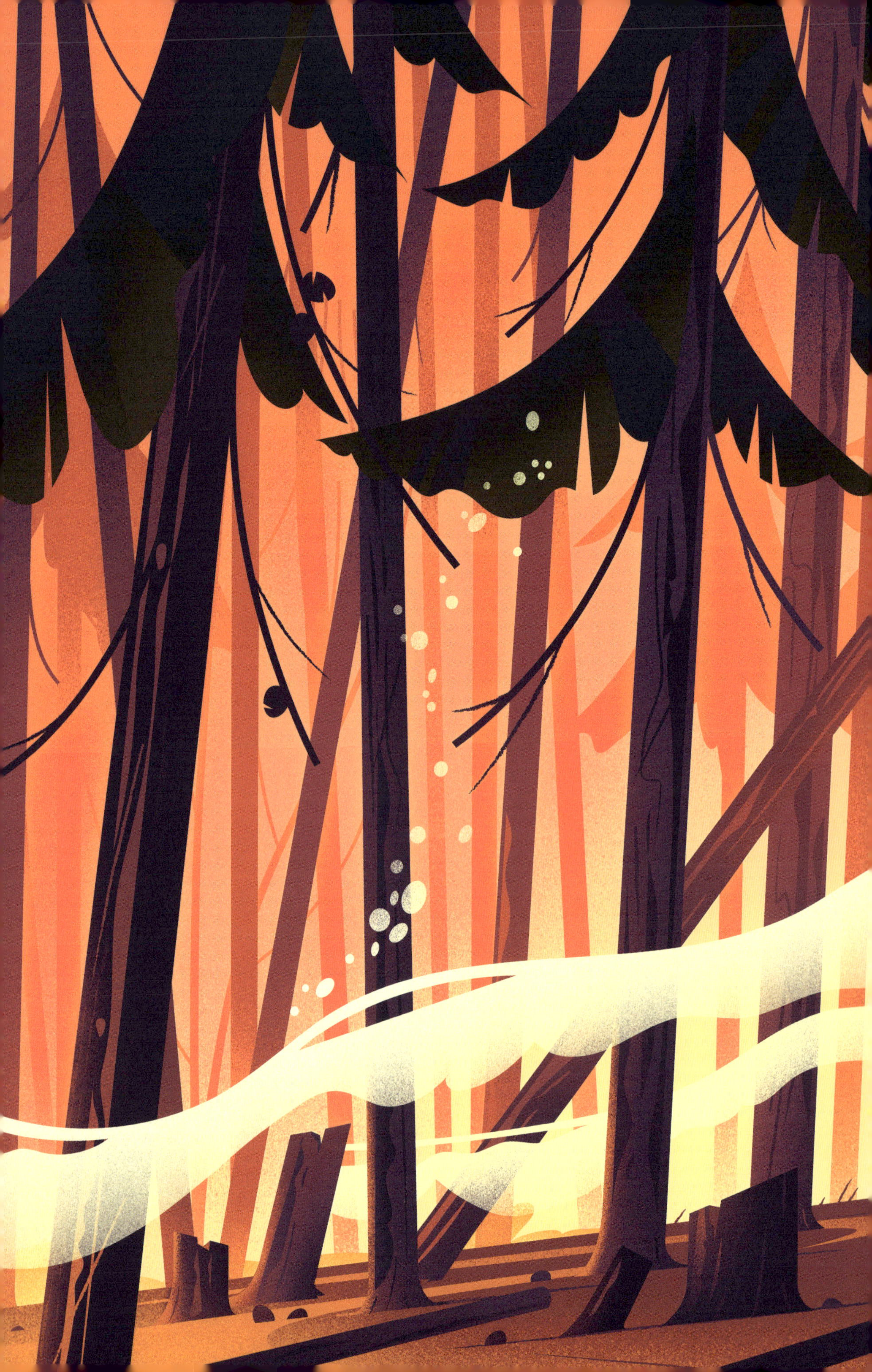

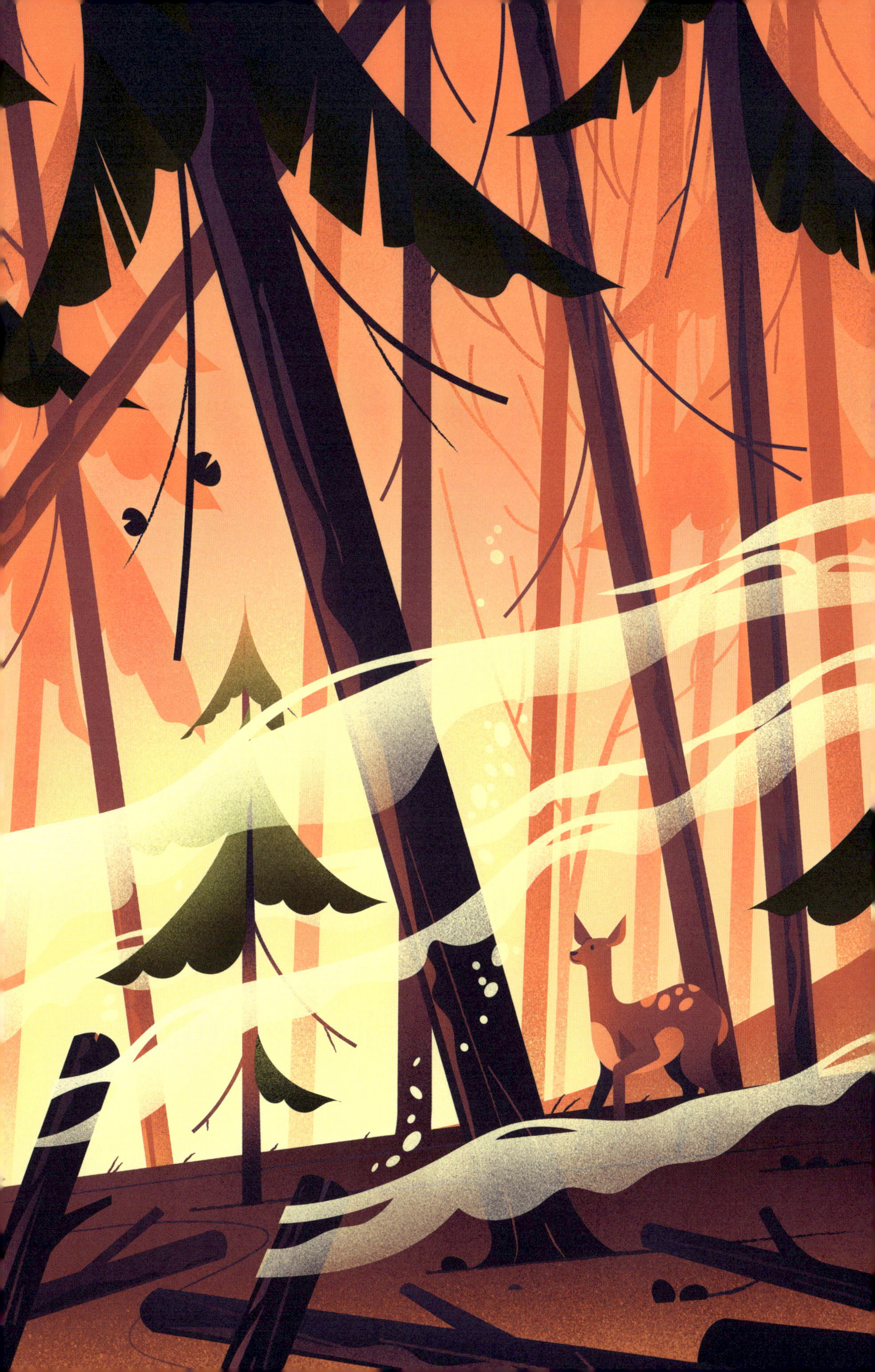

all fired up

Summer heat waves and fires are the sworn enemies of most plants. But for some ambassadors of the plant world, the extreme heat is synonymous with tactical flight. Fiery and merciless, they even take advantage of a blaze to start on new odysseys...

1. WOODY PEAR
Xylomelum angustifolium • x 1,5
Protected by its thick fireproof suit, the winged seed waits patiently for fire to pass before making an escape.

2. SPRUCE
Picea abies • x 1
Over 300 million years, spruce cones have had time to perfect their dispersion strategy.

3. MOUNTAIN DEVIL
Lambertia formosa • x 2
When surrounded by flames, this fruit opens its beak wide to release its 2 seeds.

4. ROSE BANKSIA
Banksia laricina • x 1
The bushfires in Australia's arid regions awaken the banksia's fiery temperament.

5. ROCK ROSE
Cistus • x 4
In summer, this Mediterranean plant emits an inflammable cloud useful in its reproduction.

47 all fired up

x1 *Cedrus atlantica*

48 all fired up

· ATLAS CEDAR ·

the conifer rose

Around 300 million years ago, the vast forests covering the globe saw the emergence of the first large conifers, recognizable by their cones and fine needles. The Atlas cedar is a worthy descendant of this long lineage. To survive the ages, it has adapted itself to cold and drought. Its cones, sensitive to temperature variations, disintegrate with the heat of summer. One by one, the scales, skillfully interwoven in a spiral like the petals of a rose, break off to release the seeds.

Sequoiadendron giganteum x 1

49 all fired up

• GIANT SEQUOIA •
the miniature giant

One of the greatest representatives of the plant world is a mythical sequoia known as General Sherman. This majestic tree, which is 85 meters tall, reigns over the Sierra Nevada. Who would believe that it was born more than 2,000 years ago out of a tiny seed weighing hardly 6 grams? Each of its many little cones contains more than 230 of them! This sage of the forest also knows how to wait for its cones to ripen in the intense heat before releasing thousands of miniature, sleeping giants.

x1 *Pinus halepensis*

50 all fired up

• ALEPPO PINE •

wooden fortress

In the pine forests of the Ottoman Empire, a crackling sound echoes from the tops of the trees. It is the scales of the pine cones, previously sealed with resin, expanding, and bursting under the force of summer. In the case of fire, the pine nuts—true wooden fortresses—protect every seed in their kingdom from the blaze. They can wait for years after the flames have passed before finally releasing their winged seeds. Only the strongest will carry on the torch of their elders.

Picea mariana

• BLACK SPRUCE •
a fragile balance

It's the heart of winter, and a thick blanket of white covers the immense black spruce forests that line the Artic Circle. Every 400 years, these exceptionally resilient trees regulate themselves through the great fires that engulf the forest. Unfortunately, global warming is making these megafires more frequent, threatening to upset this fragile balance. Every summer, firefighters have to struggle relentlessly to contain the flames and defend this precious heritage.

Banksia menziesii

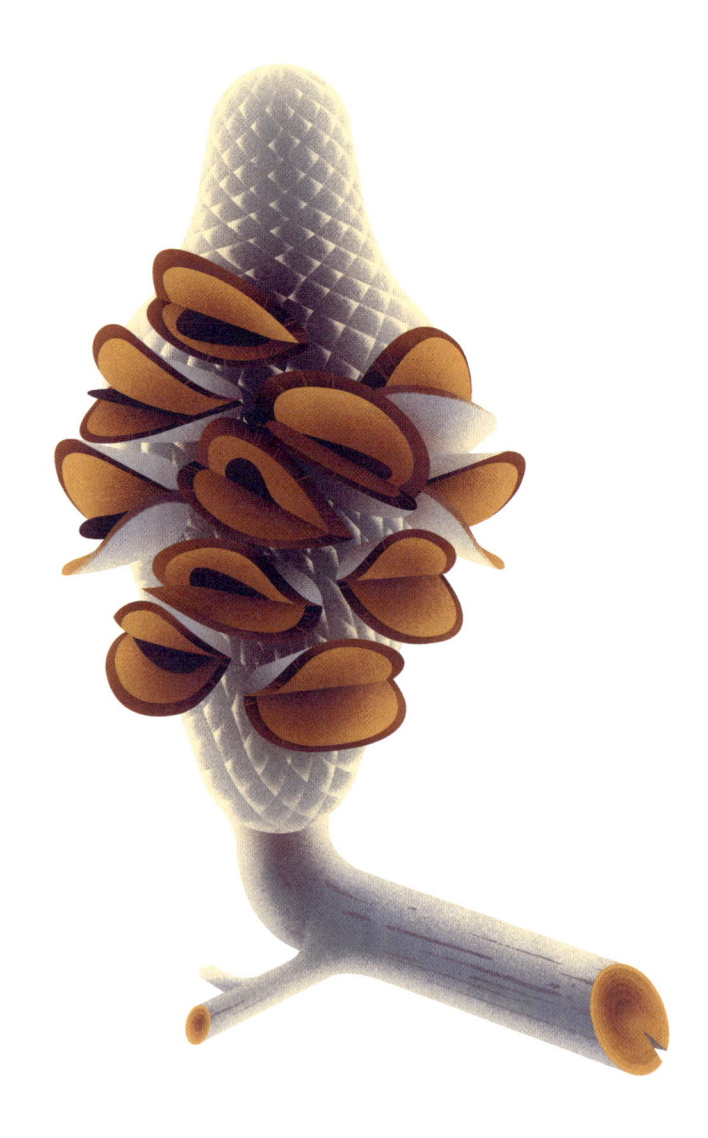

• FIREWOOD BANKSIA •
the phoenix plant

Every year, bushfires caused by lightning spread uncontrolled across Australia. While wildlife desperately attempts to escape the flames, the firewood banksia has a unique strategy for survival. It wisely waits for the blaze to pass. Offering its body to the raging inferno, it stands against the scourge and opens its valves. Winged seeds, waiting to disperse, burst forth. The shrub, partly consumed, will soon be reborn from its ashes—like a phoenix.

Casuarina collina — x 2

53   all fired up

• IRONWOOD •
pioneer of burnt lands

In the woodlands of New Caledonia, there is a cunning tree that knows how to work together with fire to survive. This opportunist seizes its chance as soon as the flames arrive. The ironwood will do anything to be the first to colonize the devastated landscape. It waits, warming up until the furnace has reached 200°C... Then it's off in a flash! It opens the scales on its cones, and its seeds, carried by the currents of hot air, have free rein over the cleared land to flourish.

x 1,5   *Eucalyptus globulus*

· BLUE GUM ·

oil to fire

Who would believe that some trees are arsonists? At the height of summer, when the heat beats down on California, this eucalyptus tree has an impressively cunning way to proliferate: it releases flammable oils. The flame-resistant tree creates gigantic blazes that keep the competition at bay. In the heat of the moment, it spreads out its thousands of tiny seeds. Though only a few will survive these extreme conditions, they will be enough to sustain the species.

Leucadendron argenteum x 3

55 all fired up

· SILVER TREE ·

green fire

The aboriginal peoples of the extreme tip of Africa possess a precious ancestral skill: taming fire. When winter approaches in the Southern Hemisphere, they masterfully set fire to the vegetation. This regenerates the land and promotes biodiversity. The silver tree needs the repeated passage of flames to renew itself! As soon as it is given the green light, it releases its seeds, which fall, spinning like tops, onto the smoldering ground. This perpetuates the cycle and preserves the ecosystem.

Callistemon citrinus

• CRIMSON BOTTLEBRUSH •
sinister fragrance

With a temperament as red-hot as the eucalyptus, the bottlebrush also likes to play with fire. In the torrid Australian climate, it is scented with a strong lemony essence capable of setting everything ablaze. When the flames finally break out, each capsule firmly attached to its branch explodes. A cloud of tiny seeds is released. Awakened from their deep slumber by the stifling heat, they germinate in the still-glowing ashes.

57 all fired up

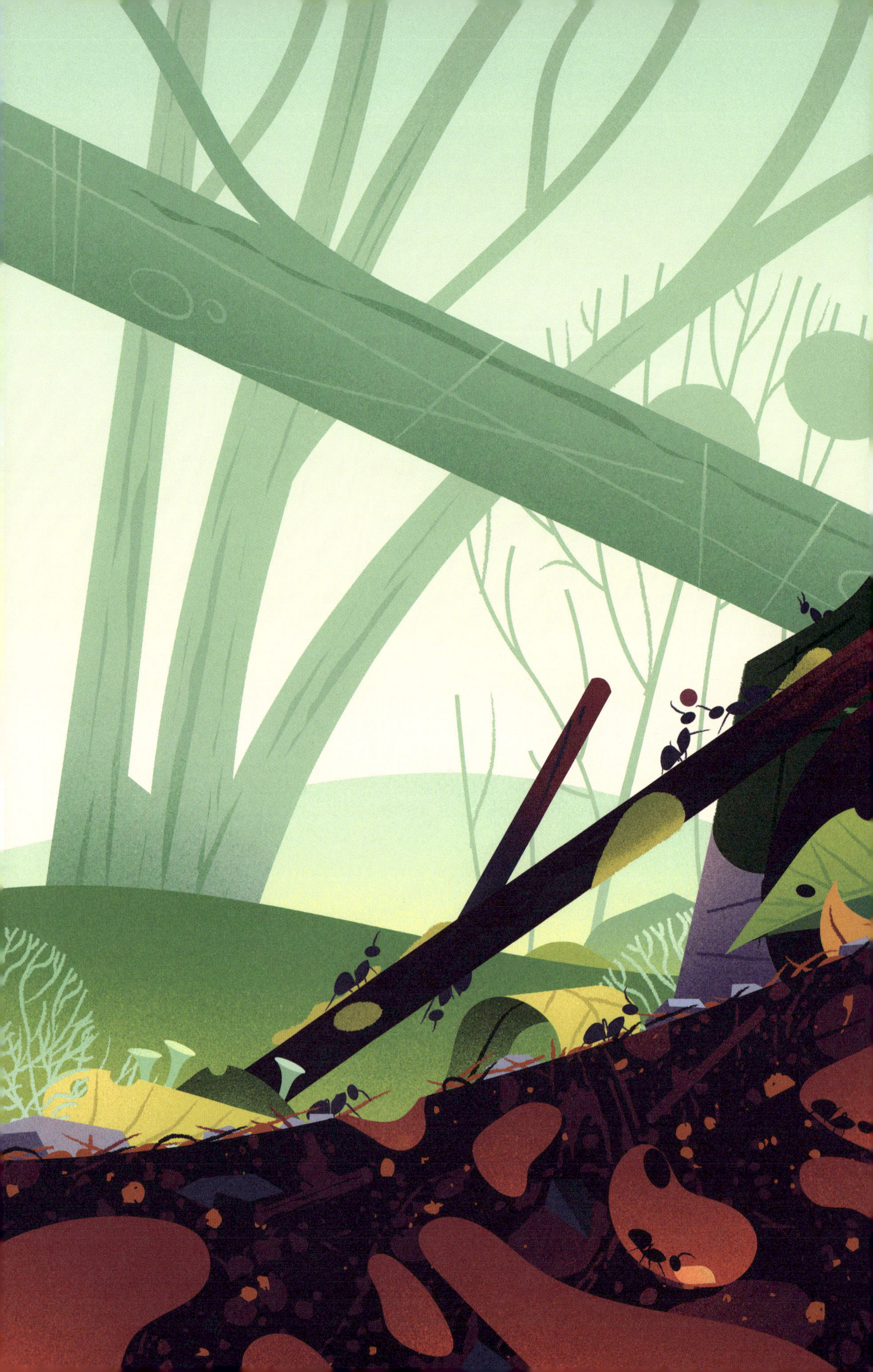

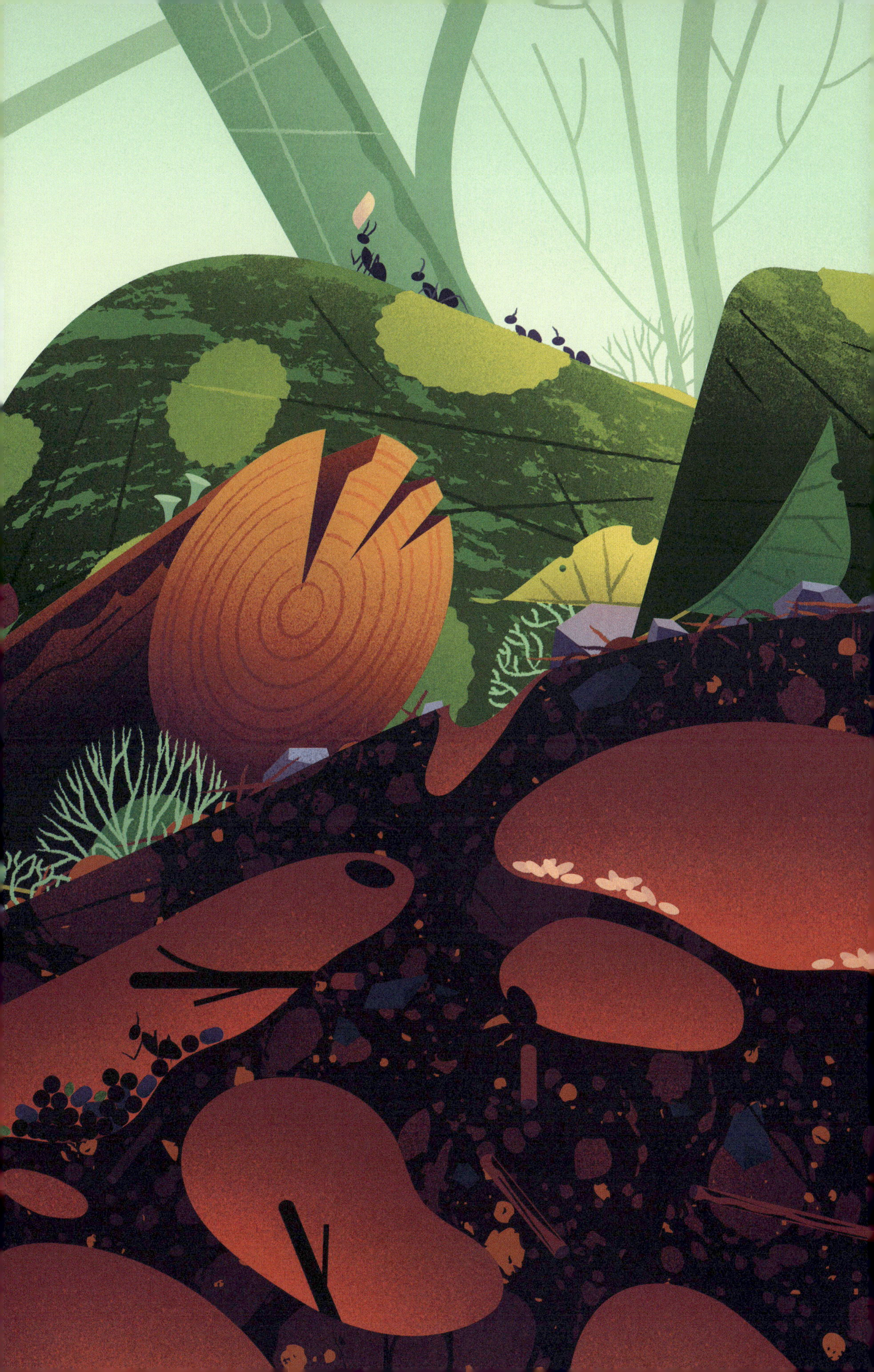

small steps, big deal

"Be kind whene'er you can, should be your creed," wrote Jean de La Fontaine, "There's none so small but you his aid may need." Several plants have understood this well and signed a pact with their friends, the ants. In exchange for transportation, the seeds offer tasty treats that guarantee the future of all the colony.

1. BLEEDING HEART
Dicentra spectabilis • x 25
Its heart-shaped flower produces seeds that are topped with a tantalizing gelatinous sap.

2. LARGE MEDITERRANEAN SPURGE
Euphorbia characias • x 30
The spurge produces over 1,000 seeds with their nourishing nectar—enough to entice the entire colony.

3. SNOWDROP
Galanthus nivalis • x 50
Several ants are needed to remove the tasty jelly covering a single seed.

4. HAIRY WOODRUSH
Luzula pilosa • x 40
Some ants can transport these seeds up to 180 meters—a colossal distance when compared with their size!!

5. BLOODROOT
Sanguinaria canadensis • x 20
The dispersal of bloodroot seeds relies on ants. Without them, this floral species would disappear!

61 small steps, big deal

x 1,5 *Helleborus foetidus*

• BEAR'S FOOT •

an exchange of services

The bear's foot and the clan of red ants have set up an exchange of services. These seeds have a nutritious growth that the transporters really like. As soon as they are picked up, the seeds are taken back home whole. The pulp is then separated and passed on to the nursery to feed the many larvae of the colony. The seeds, on the other hand, are discarded in the area dedicated to refuse disposal, which provides the ideal conditions to germinate. That's how it works!

Chelidonium majus   x 45

63   small steps, big deal

• GREATER CELANDINE •

an involuntary pact

A delicate plant lies between the stones of a wall. How did it get there? A black garden ant passed by and dropped it while it was just a tiny speck. After carrying it a few meters, the ant feasted on the seed's sugary appendage and then went on its way ... leaving the seed to its fate. Unknowingly, a pact had been honored on that day. The ant was satisfied, and the greater celandine could flourish.

Centaurea cyanus

• CORNFLOWER •

ant bread

It's harvest time! A battalion of granivorous ants is set to transport cornflower seeds. Positioned in single file, these dedicated workers form gigantic lanes of traffic. In the anthill, the collected seeds are first stored in moisture-proof chambers. They are then mashed and transformed into "ant bread": a real delicacy at the dinner party! The forgotten seeds alone may one day germinate.

Viola odorata x 27

65 small steps, big deal

• SWEET VIOLET •
a crest on the head

At the end of winter, while the flora and fauna are still partially asleep, an elegant little flower blooms low to the ground. Discreet, stealthy ants get busy. They go about their errands and gather mushrooms, insects, and violet seeds. This seed, graciously offered, is twice as large as the ant... But it would take more than that to discourage an ant! With its strong mandibles, the diligent though small creature grabs the seed by its crest and drags it back to the anthill.

Buxus sempervirens

small steps, big deal

• BOXWOOD •

an intoxicating ruse

In summer, under the blue skies of Provence's shrublands, the boxwood perfumes the landscape. A slimy syrup pearls from the surface of its little fruits. Ants, drawn by the perfumed flavors, wait expectantly for the fruit to release its large, shiny seeds to take them back to the colony. But, in reality, these seeds have little nutritional value and only need a free ride. What a clever plant! The enticed ants will only understand a little too late that they have been fooled...

Acacia cyclops   x 10

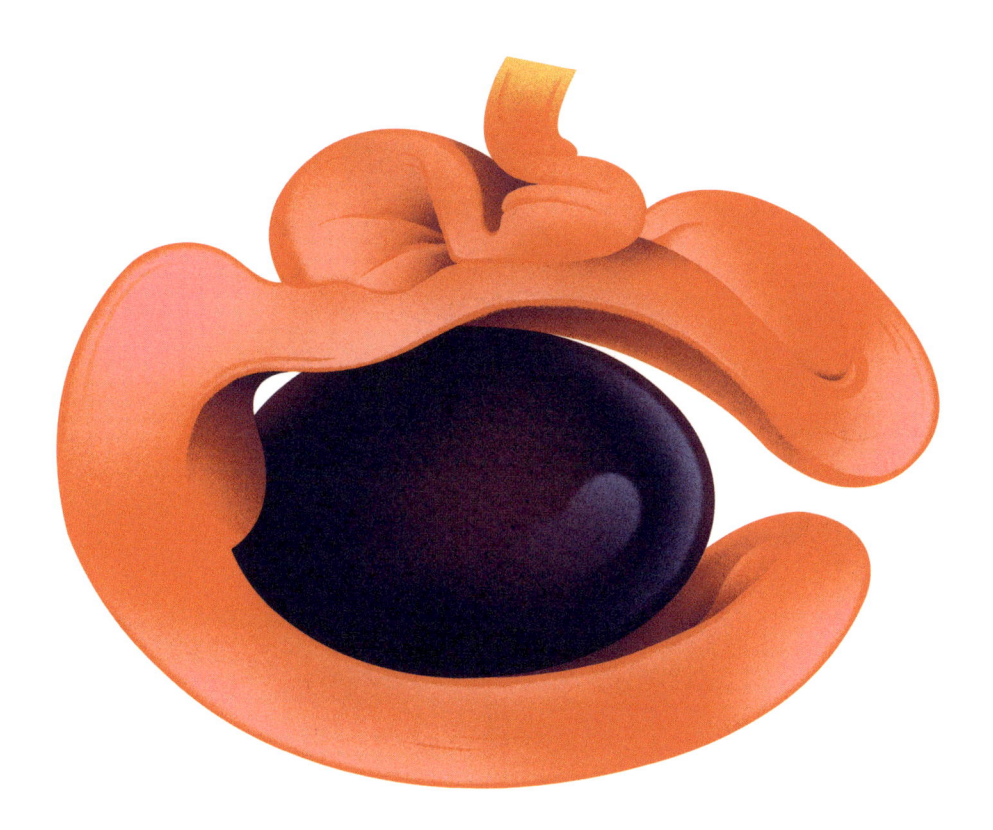

67   small steps, big deal

• COASTAL WATTLE •

blood red

The arid lands of Tasmania are home to terrible giant ants. These warmongering little creatures are crazy about the red-rimmed oval seeds of the wattle or acacia. These seeds are reminiscent of the bloody eye of the Cyclops blinded by Ulysses. But beware! While this color is mainly intended to attract birds, these ants are formidable warriors and ready to fight for their piece of the cake. Venomous and aggressive, they pounce and bite anything that craves their provisions.

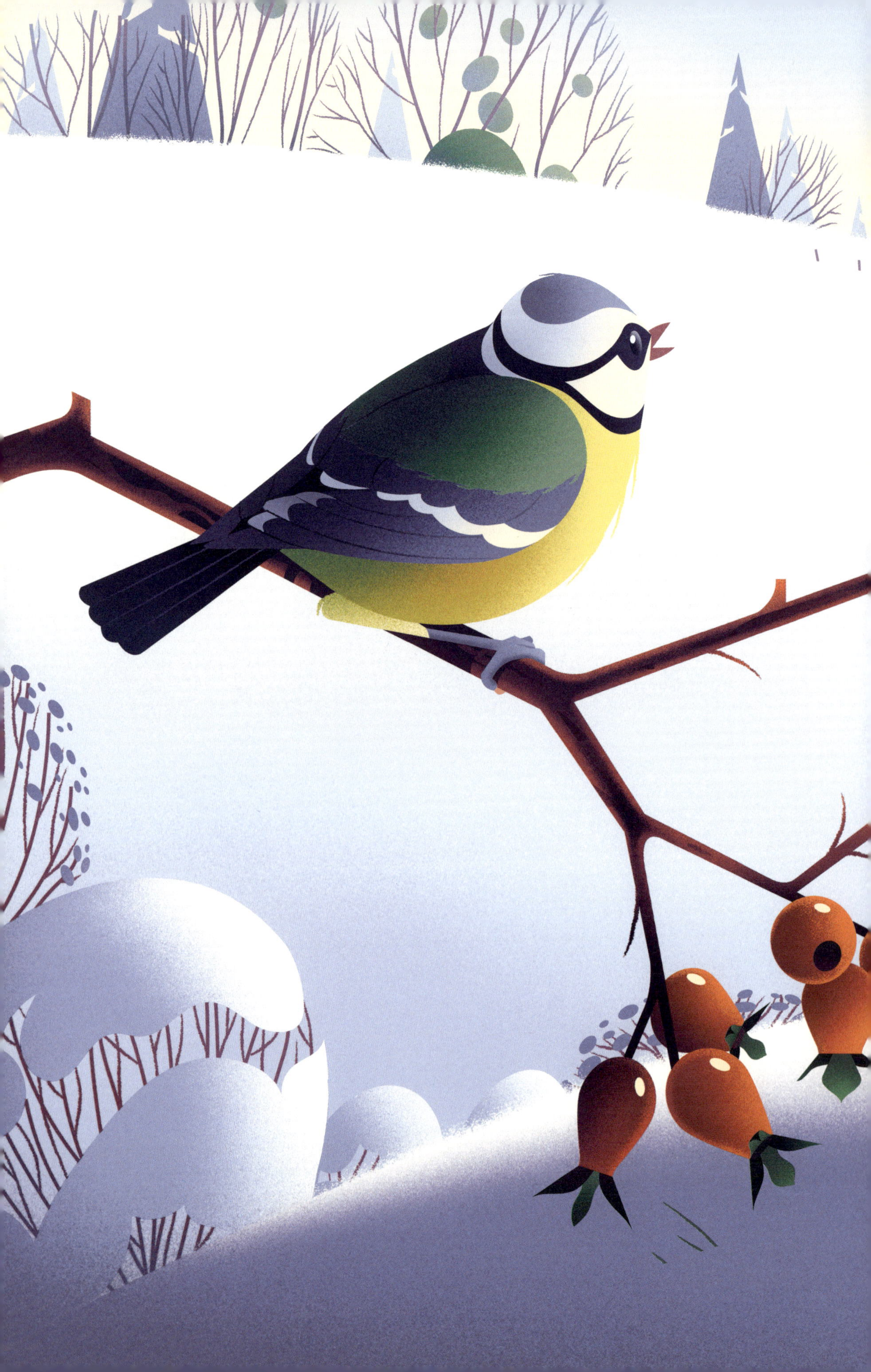

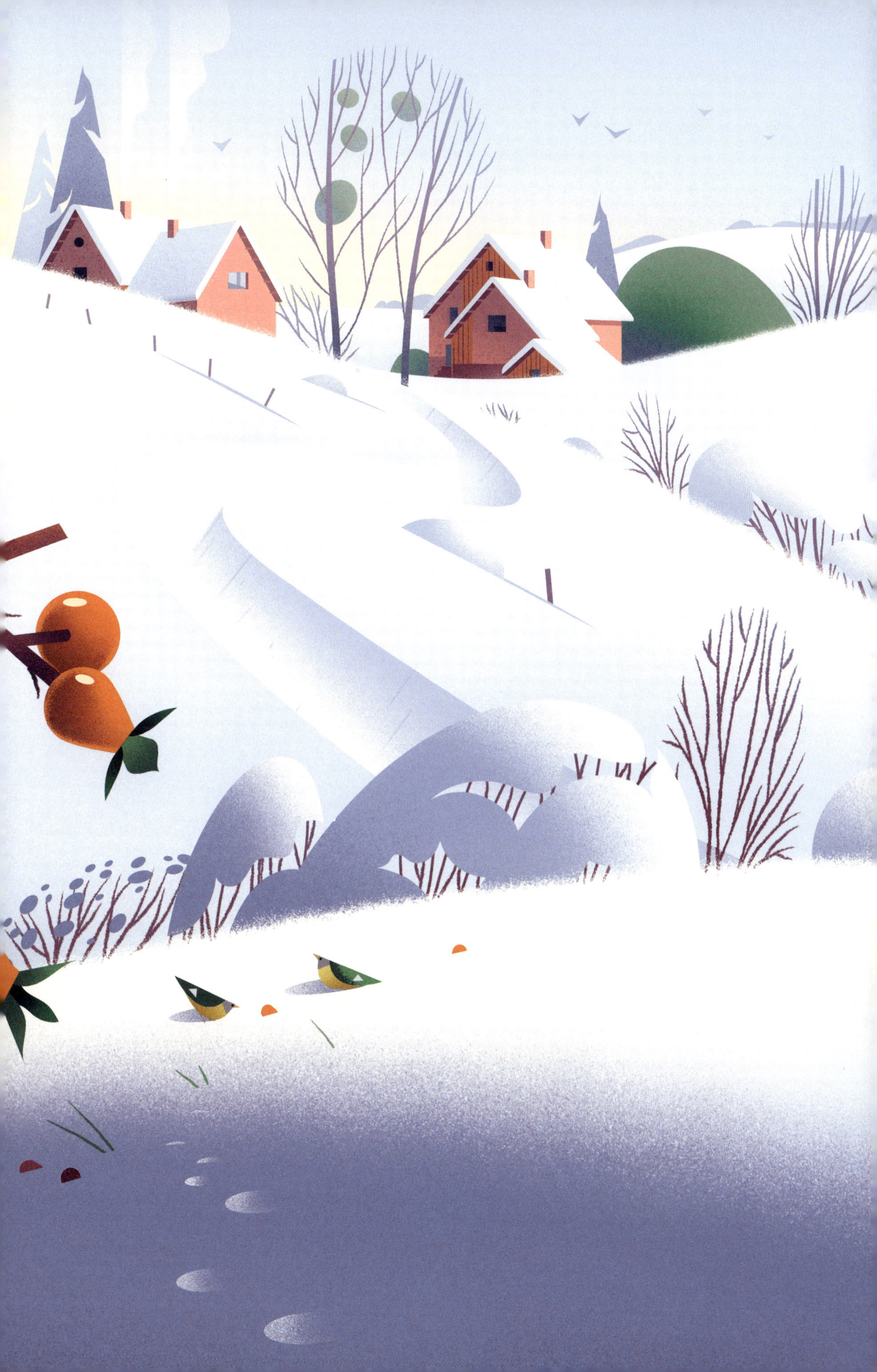

winging it

Some seeds are surprisingly mischievous. Before setting out on their epic journey, they recruit feathered friends. Attracted by the tasty appearance of the colored fruits, the birds swallow the seeds and become unknowing accomplices in their getaway...

1. ITALIAN ARUM
Arum italicum • x 1

These scarlet berries are an attractive lure for undergrowth dwellers.

2. DOG ROSE
Rosa canina • x 3

In the bird kingdom, the bright color of this fruit is a sign of good health.

3. ELDERBERRY
Sambucus • x 1,5

These juicy berries provide energy to migratory birds before they depart.

4. BIRD OF PARADISE
Strelitzia reginae • x 3,5

With its British guardsman's cap, this jaunty seed is the delight of many South African birds.

5. SWISS PINE
Pinus cembra • x 2

One bird, the crossbill, excels in dislodging these seeds from their cones.

6. PEONY
Paeonia • x 1

As they open, the pods reveal their red and black finery, which catches the eye of birds.

7. SPINDLE TREE
Euonymus • x

When famine strikes, the spindle draws attention with its fruits.

8. WATER LIANA
Tetracera billardierei • x 10

Snuggled in its ruddy nest, the seed awaits the passage of parakeets.

71 winging it

x 1,5 *Afzelia Africana*

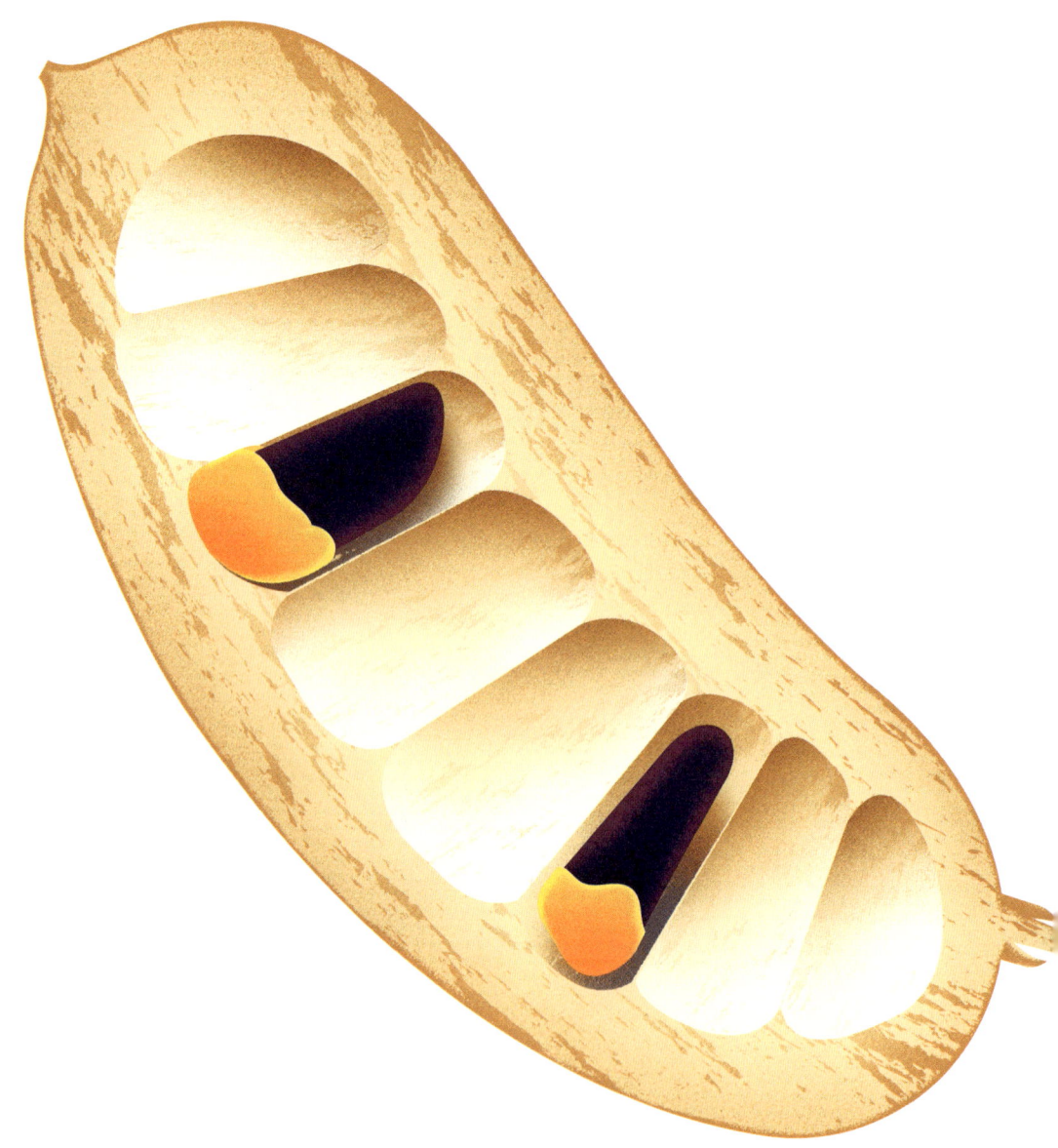

• DOUSSI •

an expert safecracker

A majestic creature with multicolored plumage lives on the edge of the savannah: the hornbill. This strange bird is an expert safecracker. When feeling peckish, it does not hesitate to assail the fruit of the doussi: a real locked safe. With its long, helmeted beak, it splits the tough pod in half to steal the seeds. It then grabs them by their orange headdress, eats the pulp, and disposes of the rest immediately. In this way, the hornbill unknowingly takes part in their dispersal.

73 winging it

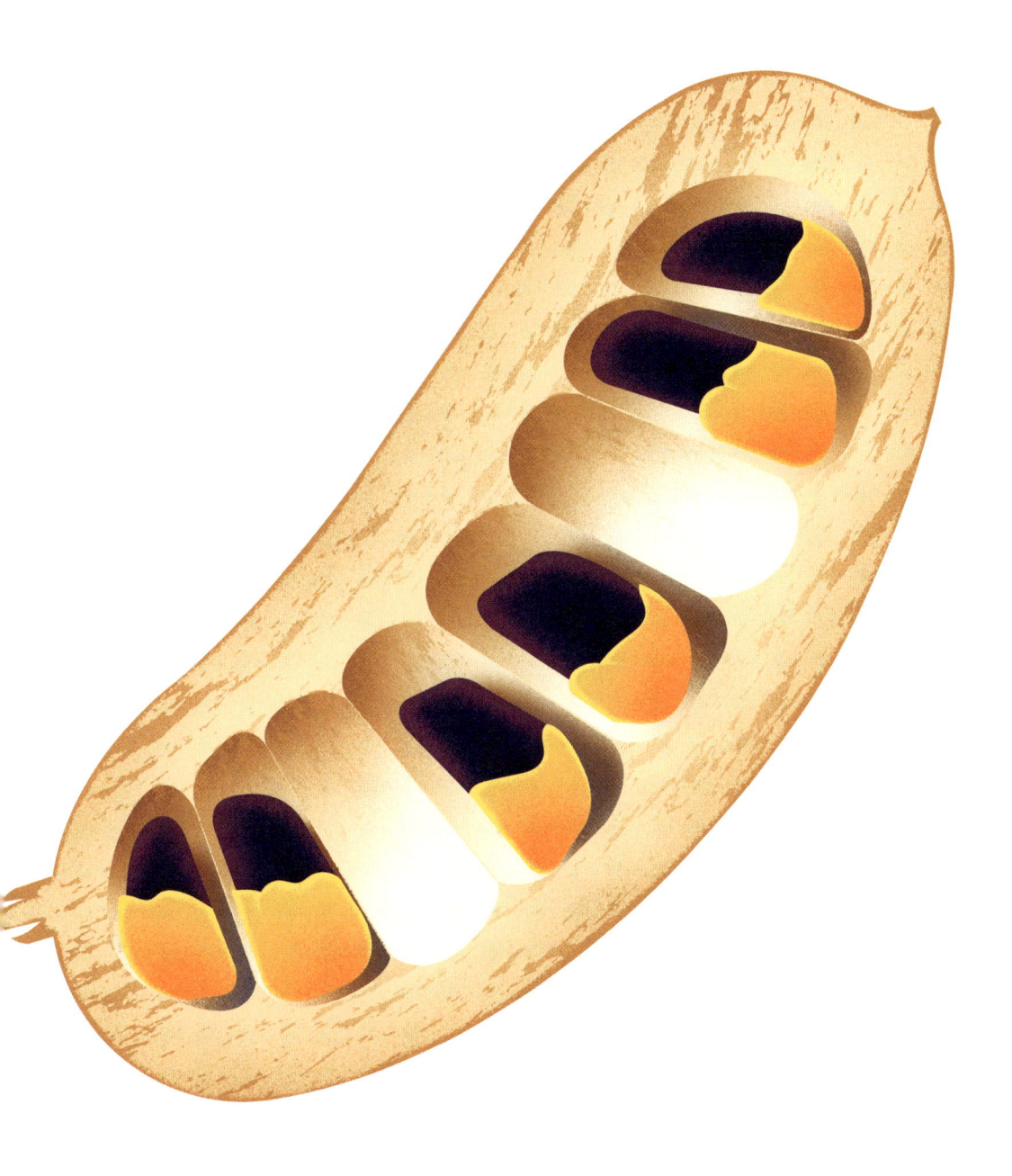

· YEW ·

surprise package

Like many other fruit plants, the yew has endowed its seeds with a tasty, nutritious package. This is to satisfy the appetite of the local fauna. What a strange idea—wanting to be eaten! But the plant is not crazy. As long as the seeds have not reached maturity, the flesh remains green, acidic, and hard in order to hide itself and safeguard its prize. When the weather improves, they will be decked out in vibrant colors and the birds are attracted to join in this great maneuver orchestrated by nature

Coriaria myrtifolia x 2,5

75 winging it

• REDOUL •
intimate travel

Under the scorching heat of Andalucia, a blackbird eats the small, fleshy berries of the redoul, which is toxic to other feathered animals. But these two have signed a secret pact. By becoming edible for this little bird, the seed will go on a fabulous intestinal journey! And for the seeds, it's a real godsend! The blackbird's digestive juices will soften the hard shell without damaging it so that, when it wakes up among the droppings, all it will have to do is establish its new kingdom.

Viscum album

• MISTLETOE •

ingenious parasite

Fruit is scarce in winter's bare forests and the thrush's belly cries out for food. Only an ingenious parasitic plant, clinging to a branch, bears fruit. The tiny mistletoe berries, coated with slimy filaments, are the thrush's favorite meal. After a brief visit to the digestive tract, the seeds emerge, held together by a thread, like a rosary, which, as it falls, will cling firmly to a branch. A real pot of glue that will give birth to a new plant.

Euonymus cornutus   x 2

77   winging it

• FIVE-HORNED SPINDLE •

providential food

Wintry weather has arrived on the Tibetan plateau. For the spindle's pods, it is time to open up and offer their magnificent bright-orange seeds to fruit-eating birds. In the eyes of these aesthetes, this color is synonymous with a providential source of energy. But beware, it is a matter of give and take. In exchange for its nutritive contribution, the toxic seed must be digested in a hurry; if not, watch out for its laxative effect! Expelled intact among the bird's excrement, it can then germinate.

Ravenala madagascariensis

• TRAVELER'S TREE •
the savior of madagascar

In the heart of Madagascar's tropical jungle stands a lifesaving "palm tree" unlike any other: the traveler's tree. Its abundant, drinkable sap has saved more than one off-course explorer or traveler in need. In collaboration with various members of the animal kingdom, this plant contributes to the balance of an entire ecosystem. Its flowers attract lemurs who, in return, ensure pollination. And its seeds, covered in a deep blue envelope, captivate the birds that then scatter them.

Vaccinium myrtillus   x 8

79   winging it

• BLUEBERRY •

midnight berry

We often ignore that birds have exceptional eyesight: one of the most powerful in the animal kingdom! They can even perceive ultraviolet light! And that is especially useful for finding food in the undergrowth... And so, they can distinguish the small blackish blue berries better than anyone else. The whitish film on these fruits reflects ultraviolet rays, making them brighter than ever! The birds are thus able to choose the ripest fruits for their enjoyment.

• GUARANA •

a bewitching gaze

Guarana has given rise to many indigenous legends of the Amazon. Its unusual appearance has earned it another name, "eye of the forest." Its fruits are coveted by birds. But toucans have learned to be careful. They gorge themselves on the white pulp that covers the pits, like a lychee, but avoid swallowing the seed, which is extremely high in caffeine. If one is inadvertently swallowed, the dizzy bird will be quick to spit it out as soon as digestion begins. This saves it a lot of unpleasantness...

Margaritaria nobilis x 5

• BASTARD HOGBERRY •
fool's gold

This fleshy fruit is a marvel of adaptation. Its small beads, reflecting an iridescent blue, are actually a lure with the most beautiful effect! This physical phenomenon, similar to that of a butterfly's wings, is not at all nourishing for whomever gets hold of it. At the slightest touch, the brilliant color fades and the pulp covering the seed becomes translucent. Too late! The ignorant bird has been fooled. Without knowing it, he will be offering the seed a fine odyssey at very little cost.

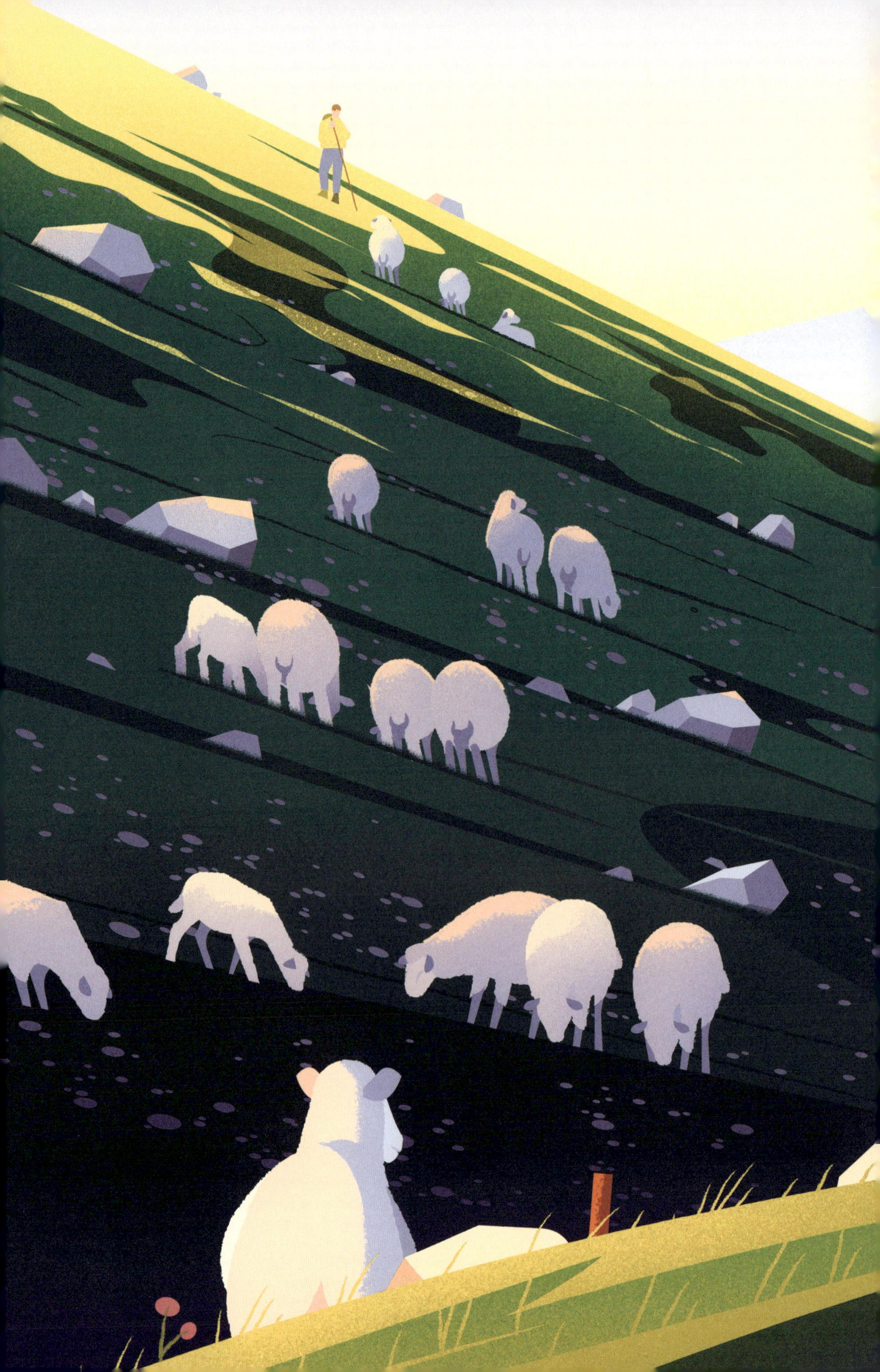

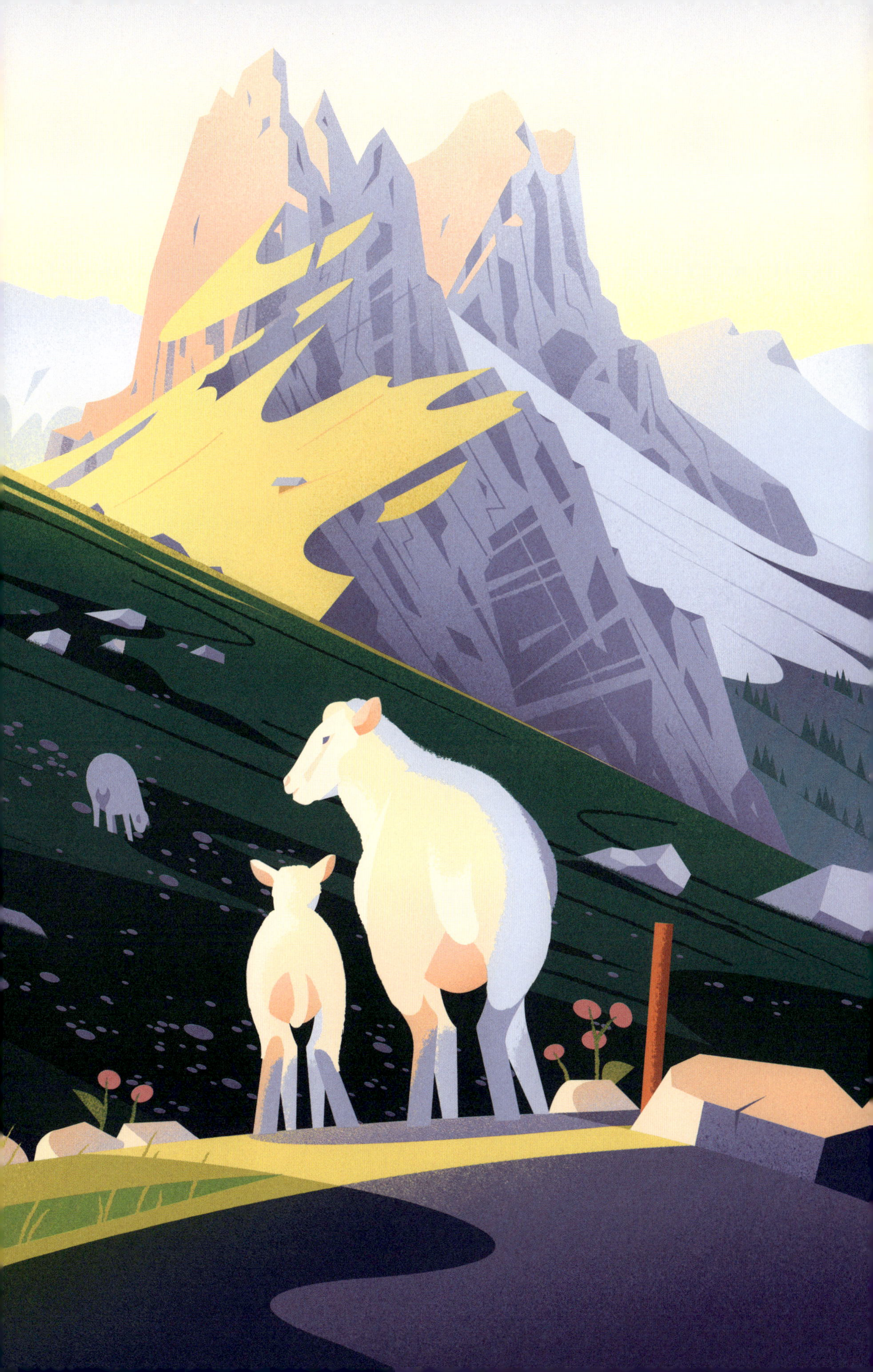

on all fours

Although birds and insects are fine companions in adventure, small and large mammals are equally as good! Clinging to a sheep's fleece or nestling in a mouse's stomach, some seeds play stowaway and roam about at the whim of their ride.

1. TICKSEED
Bidens sp. • x 12,5

With its 2 needle-like teeth, the tickseed hooks itself to fur.

2. CLEAVER
Galium aparine • x 5

These small fruits bristling with hairs stick to anything that moves!

3. STICKLEWORT
Agrimonia eupatoria • x 12

With its hooked barb, its fruit clings to a horse's flowing mane.

4. SOUR CHERRY
Prunus cerasus • x 3

Foxes feed on cherries and spread clumps of the undigested pits.

5. MARIGOLD
Calendula • x 2,5

This carefree seed can cling to hair or else be carried along by the wind.

6. HAZELNUT
Corylus avellana • x 2,5

Squirrels love to collect hazelnuts and store them in their hiding places.

7. DEVIL'S CLAW
Harpagophytum procumbens • x 1

The hook-like fangs of this fruit are dreadful when they plant themselves in your skin.

85 on all fours

x 1,5 *Magnolia*

on all fours

· MAGNOLIA ·

horn of plenty

The very first flowering plants appeared in the lush jungle of the Jurassic Period. A revolution! Pollinating insects thrived. Giant reptiles and fruit-eating dinosaurs coexisted peacefully to share the extraordinary horn of plenty provided by nature. And, as early as in the Cretaceous Period, the magnolia's ancestor displayed its seeds wrapped in attractive bright red film to whet the appetites of the colossi. This strategy paid off and the magnolia is still with us today!

Enterolobium cyclocarpum x 1

87 on all fours

• ELEPHANT'S EAR •

indispensable colossus

A kind of mastodon called a gomphothere lived 20 million years ago. Crossing the path of this pachyderm was a blessing for the guanacaste (or elephant's ear) tree. The beast's powerful jaws and slow digestion favored the germination of the tough seeds. Expelled with its excrements, the seeds were dispersed across the supercontinent. Today, few mammals are able to cover such distances. And, sadly, the territory of this majestic tree is slowly shrinking.

x 2,5　　　　　　　　　　　　　　　　　　　　　　　　　　　*Proboscidea louisianica*

· RAM'S HORN ·
from hell

Glutinous and hairy from head to foot, this cruel plant traps flies, mosquitoes, and gnats attracted by its nauseous stench. And that is not its only Machiavellian trait... When mature, it produces dry, spiny fruits straight from hell! Armed with two exceptionally long claws, they cling viciously to the paws of large mammals and take a ride at their expense. When the suffering animal finally manages to trample them, the shell cracks open and releases dozens of seeds.

89 on all fours

x 4   *Avena fatua*

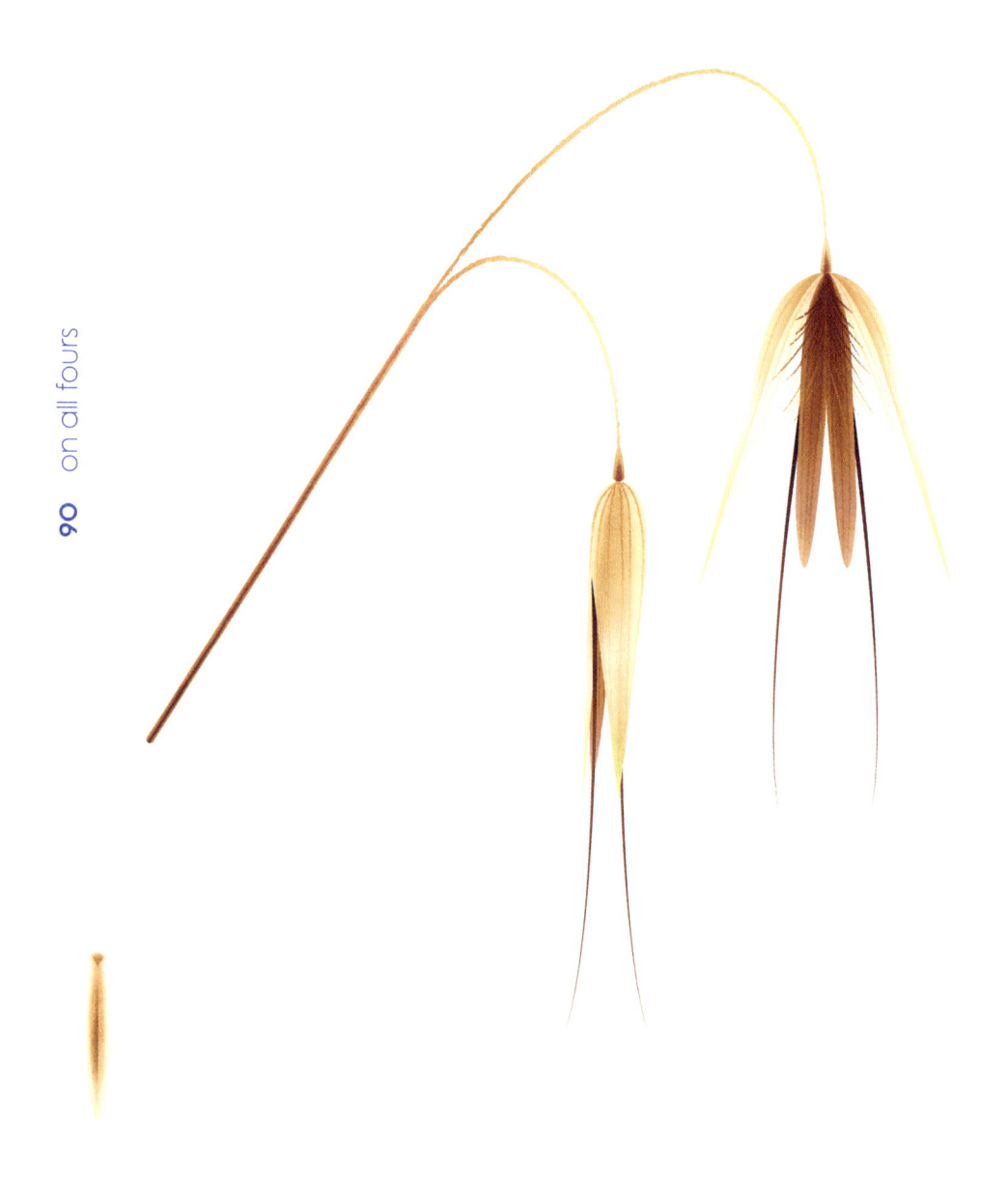

· WILD OAT ·

a mad seed

Untamed and mischievous, wild oats are everywhere in the meadows grazed by domesticated cattle. When it dreams of adventure, it uses its two long stalks like grasshopper legs to hoist itself onto the fur of a carefree mount. But if it inadvertently wriggles its way into the animal's moist snout, it twists about causing painful irritation. The animal snorts madly to get rid of the stowaway, which puts an end to its wanderlust. The epic journey has sadly been short-lived.

Desmodium canadense x 4

· CANADIAN TICK-TREFOIL ·

blasted pot of glue

Indian summer settles into the far north of Canada and the maple leaves are ablaze with color. Nestled in the dense undergrowth, the tick-trefoil has taken up residence close to a trapper's cabin. It is lying in ambush! This discreet opportunist is waiting for the hunter and his faithful four-legged companion to pass by to cling firmly to them and set out for new horizons. A real pot of glue, it is dispersed thanks to the adhesive fluff covering its delicate triangular pods.

x1 *Adansonia digitata*

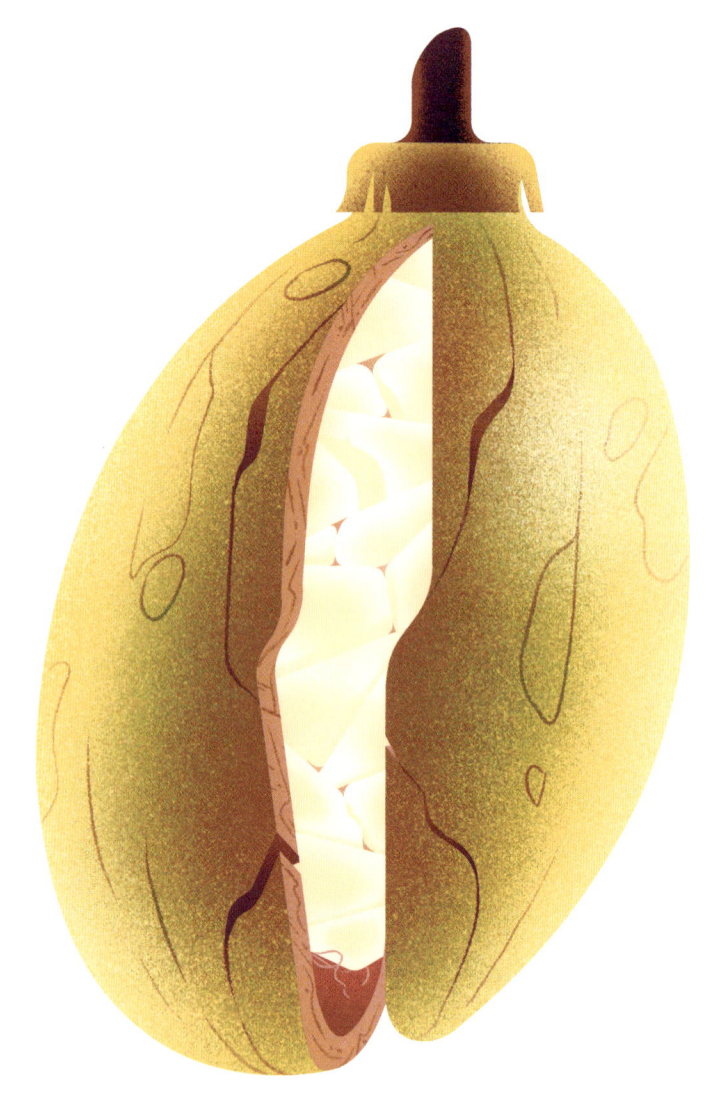

92 on all fours

· AFRICAN BAOBAB ·
tree of life

Perched in the arms of a thousand-year-old baobab, a group of baboons have taken possession of this tree of life. They watch as the inhabitants of the savannah crave their precious booty. Elephants, rhinoceroses, antelopes, ground squirrels, and even termites wait for the right moment to grab the large energizing fruits of this beneficent tree. But these primates do not like sharing. From high up, they selfishly savor the pulp that covers the seeds, as floury as dry bread … only leaving the crumbs.

Quercus ilex x 3

93 on all fours

· OAK ·

memory lapse

It's autumn! Under the oak canopy, deer and wild boar are busy preparing for winter. The squirrel is also stocking up! Foraging among the dead leaves, they find the biggest acorns they are so fond of. If there is a worm inside, it is eaten on the spot. The others are carefully buried, stored away and protected from the cold and the elements. But, sadly, the squirrel does not have the memory of an elephant ... and some forgotten hiding places will sprout into pretty little plants in spring.

x 4   *Fragaria vesca*

94   on all fours

· WILD STRAWBERRY ·

temptation of the flesh

On the green carpet of the forest, a short-legged inhabitant scurries frantically between mosses and leaves. The fieldmouse, a small rodent with a sharp sense of smell, has sniffed out the delicate scent of wild strawberries. Its fragrance and seed-riddled red flesh are a real temptation for many small animals in the undergrowth. Delicately hidden in the shadows of the foliage, the strawberry patiently bides its time… The gluttonous will feast on it and scatter the seeds along their path.

Hernandia nymphaeifolia x 1,5

• LANTERN TREE •

lanterns in the night

Every evening, a strange creature—the flying fox—appears on the coast of Madagascar. With its foxlike head and broad wings, it is one of the world's biggest bats. As soon as night falls, this nocturnal bat abandons its home and starts gathering. Due to its unrivalled sense of smell and exceptional radar, the exquisite white fruits appear like lanterns in the night to the bat. Hanging from a branch, it savors its harvest and carefully discards the large pits.

Tribulus terrestris

• DEVIL'S THORN •
the way of calvary

This creeping plant wreaks havoc all along the Mediterranean! Its starry fruits are reminiscent of the Templar cross. And it is not a good omen to cross their path. Armed with sharp, terribly resistant thorns, its fruits cling firmly to horses' hooves. This is the beginning of a real ordeal for the unfortunate mount ... It is only after a long struggle that the animal will rid itself of them and put an end to its suffering. The seeds, now scattered, can flourish.

Arctium x 5

97 on all fours

• BURDOCK •

vegetal velcro

This cheerful member of the thistle tribe is a regular on the paths bordering our fields. Who hasn't come across it? In summer, its spiny ball with tiny hooks takes advantage of long-haired travelers passing by and jumps at the chance to cling to their fur. Thus begins a wild adventure… It was while he was observing this ingenious mechanism of nature that George de Mestral invented Velcro ("vel" for *velours* or "velvet," and "cro" for *crochet* or "hook")—a fine example of biomimicry.

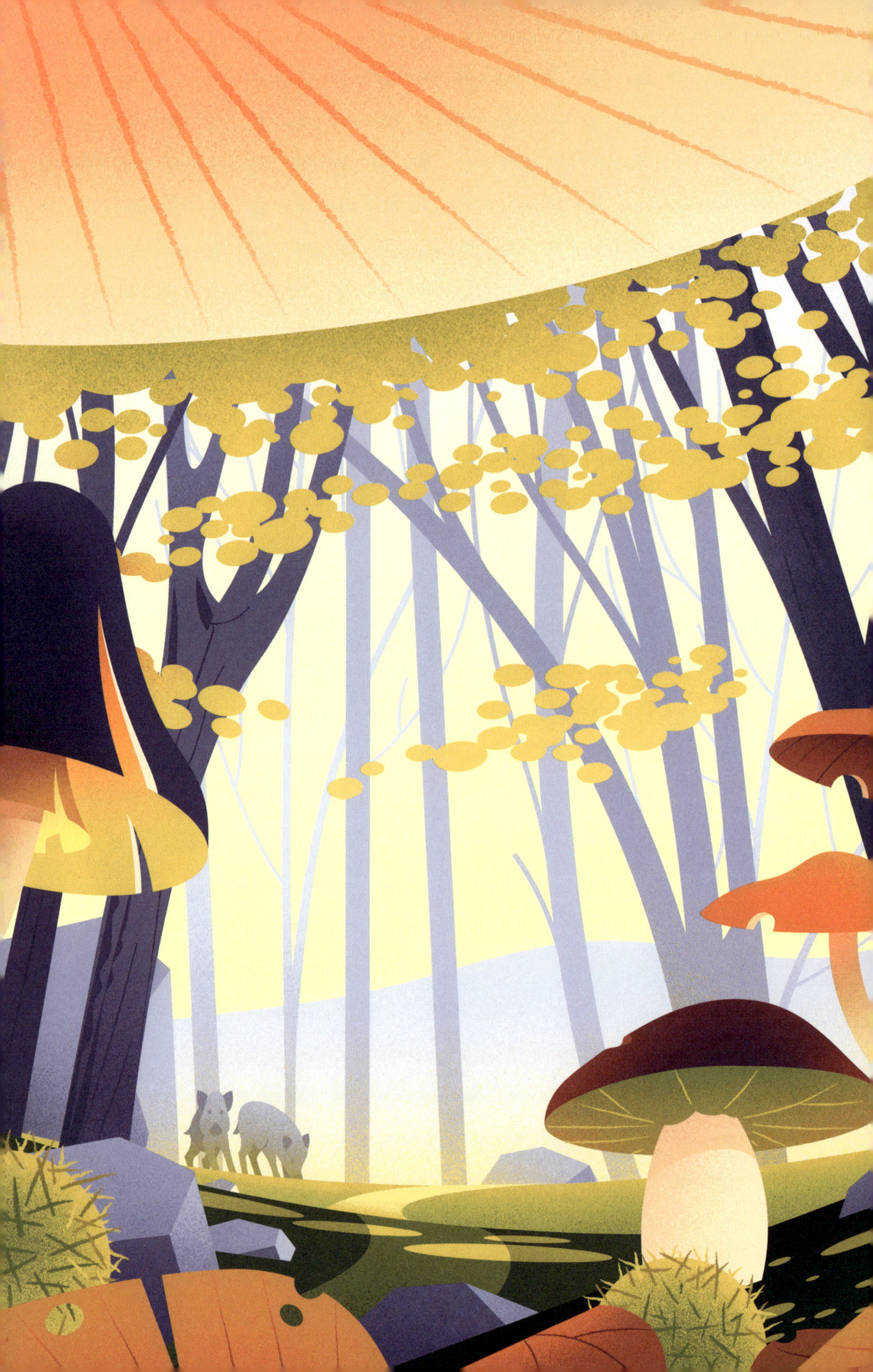

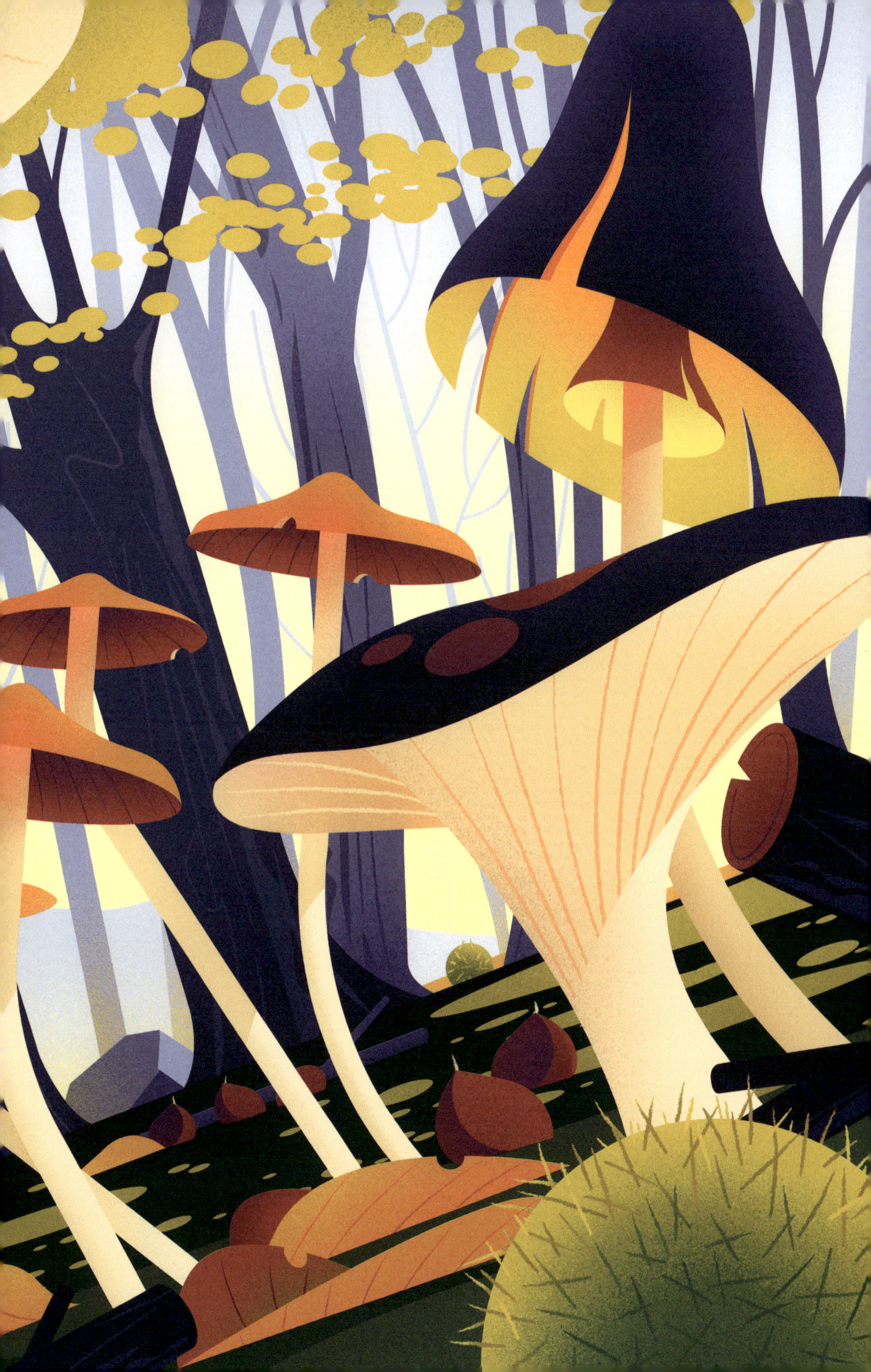

in free fall

Not very daring; these seeds do not really have the stuff of great adventurers. Taking advantage of the law of gravity, they simply let themselves fall and roll along the ground. Fortunately, Mother Nature has given them a large reserve of energy that enables them to germinate and thus guarantees their survival.

1. INCA PEANUT
Plukenetia volubilis • x 2

The Inca peanut uses its weight and the greed of animals to spread.

2. GARDEN PEA
Pisum sativum • x 2

On the ground, these small green pearls take advantage of slopes to roll and escape.

3. LENTIL
Lens culinaris • x 7,5

The nutritive flesh of these tiny seeds is an enormous source of energy.

4. HORSE CHESTNUT
Aesculus hippocastanum • x 1

This chestnut rarely ventures more than 10 meters from the tree.

5. CHICKPEA
Cicer arietinum • x 2,5

This fleshy pea knows how to dip into its resources to survive the winter and germinate.

6. BLACK HICKORY
Carya texana • x 1,5

Putting its fall to good use, the nut slips under the carpet of dead leaves and buries itself.

7. CANNONBALL TREE
Couroupita guianensis • x 0,5

Round and heavy like a cannonball—beware when this fruit falls from its tree!

101 in free fall

x 2,5 *Castanea*

102 in free fall

• CHESTNUT •

power dive

It's autumn and time for chestnut season! From the golden tops of the trees, the spiny balls plunge, one by one, drawn without resistance to the ground. Why move away when you can be sure there is good ground nearby? The most fortunate can hide under the cover of dead leaves. But they will have to be patient and wait for the return of spring before they can germinate. Sleeping all winter, those that do not wake up in good time will be doomed to rot slowly.

Juglans regia   x 2

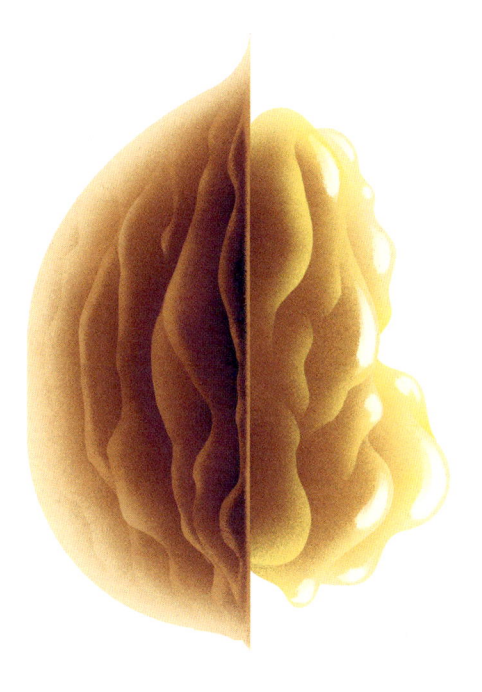

103 in free fall

• ENGLISH WALNUT •
a real brain teaser

Falling straight from the tree, a walnut attracts the attention of a winged gourmand. Can it withstand the jay's beak? The brain-shaped seed, nestled in its sturdy cranium, proves very difficult to extract. It's a real brain teaser for the bird! After several unsuccessful attempts, the jay abandons it a few meters away. For this ingenious shelled fruit, which has evolved to thwart the attacks of its predators, the trial of strength is won.

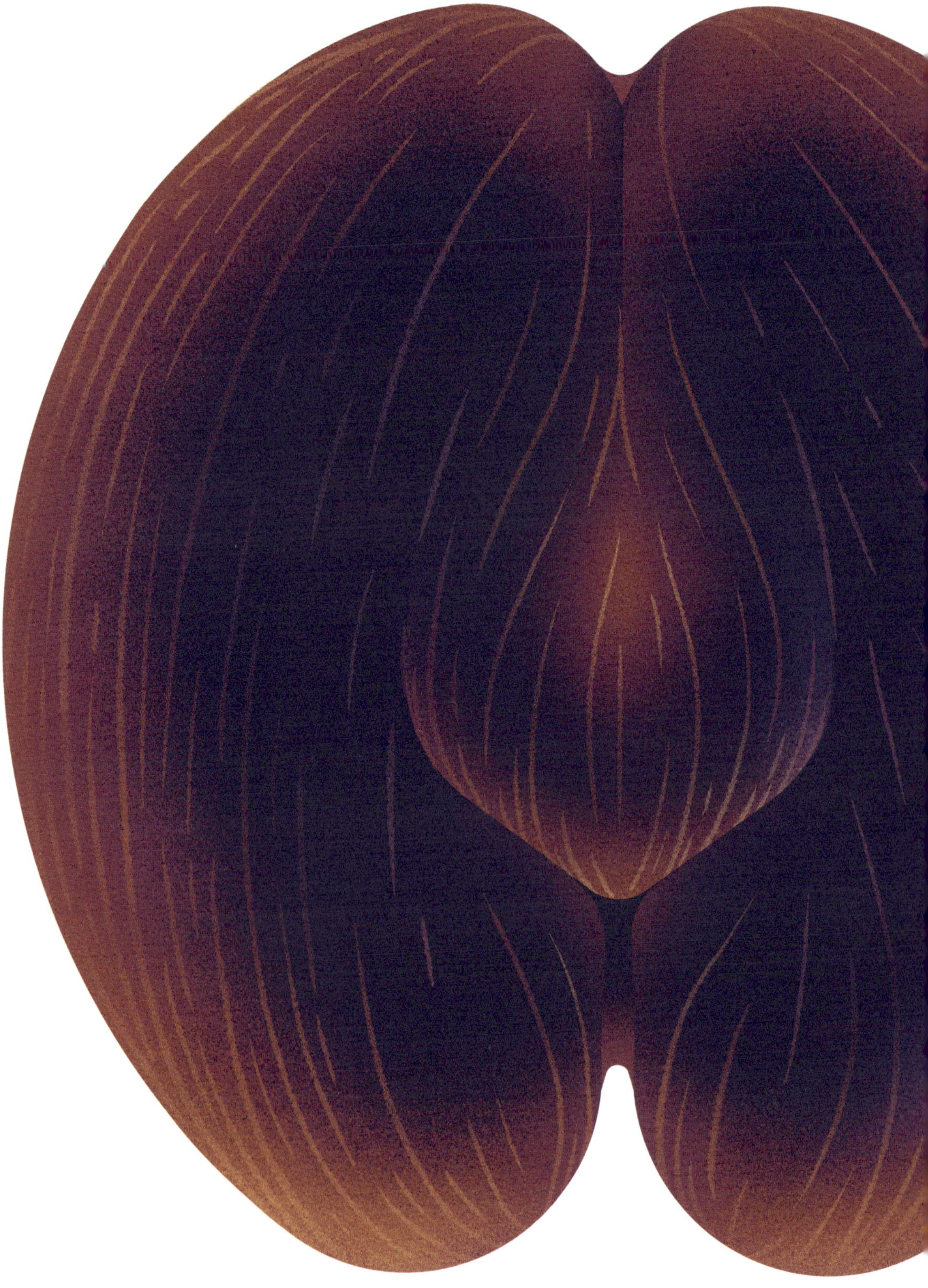

Lodoicea maldivica   x 0,5

105   in free fall

• COCO DE MER •
heavyweight champion

With its voluptuous shape and its enormous size, the fruit of the coco de mer is the largest and heaviest in the plant kingdom. Reaching 50 centimeters in length and weighing more than 20 kilograms, it's imposing. But that does not make it any less vulnerable. While its cousin, the coconut, has crossed all the oceans, the weight of this giant condemns it to short distances. Isolated on its tiny island in the middle of the Indian Ocean, its species is now threatened with extinction.

Persea americana

· AVOCADO ·

spoiled child

Vital light is really very scarce under the dense foliage of the tropical jungle... And the young trees, in the shadow of their elders, fight a merciless battle for survival. But the avocado tree, a thoughtful parent, has taken care to provide its offspring with a fine parcel of provisions. With its large pit covered by a protein-rich envelope, the spoiled child has all the nutritional reserves it could wish for. As soon as it starts growing, the little plant can dip into its bundle and treat itself to a host of snacks.

Bertholletia excelsa x 1,5

107 in free fall

· BRAZIL NUT ·

gilded cage

On the banks of the Amazon, immense nut trees jut out over the forest canopy. Their nuts fall like missiles from their 50-meter height (the equivalent of a 16-floor building). Some shatter during the bumpy landing, but most remain intact... For the seeds they contain, these armored shells are genuine gilded cages that deprive them of freedom. Abandoned there, out of sight, they begin to germinate with just a small, pierced operculum as their only window on the world.

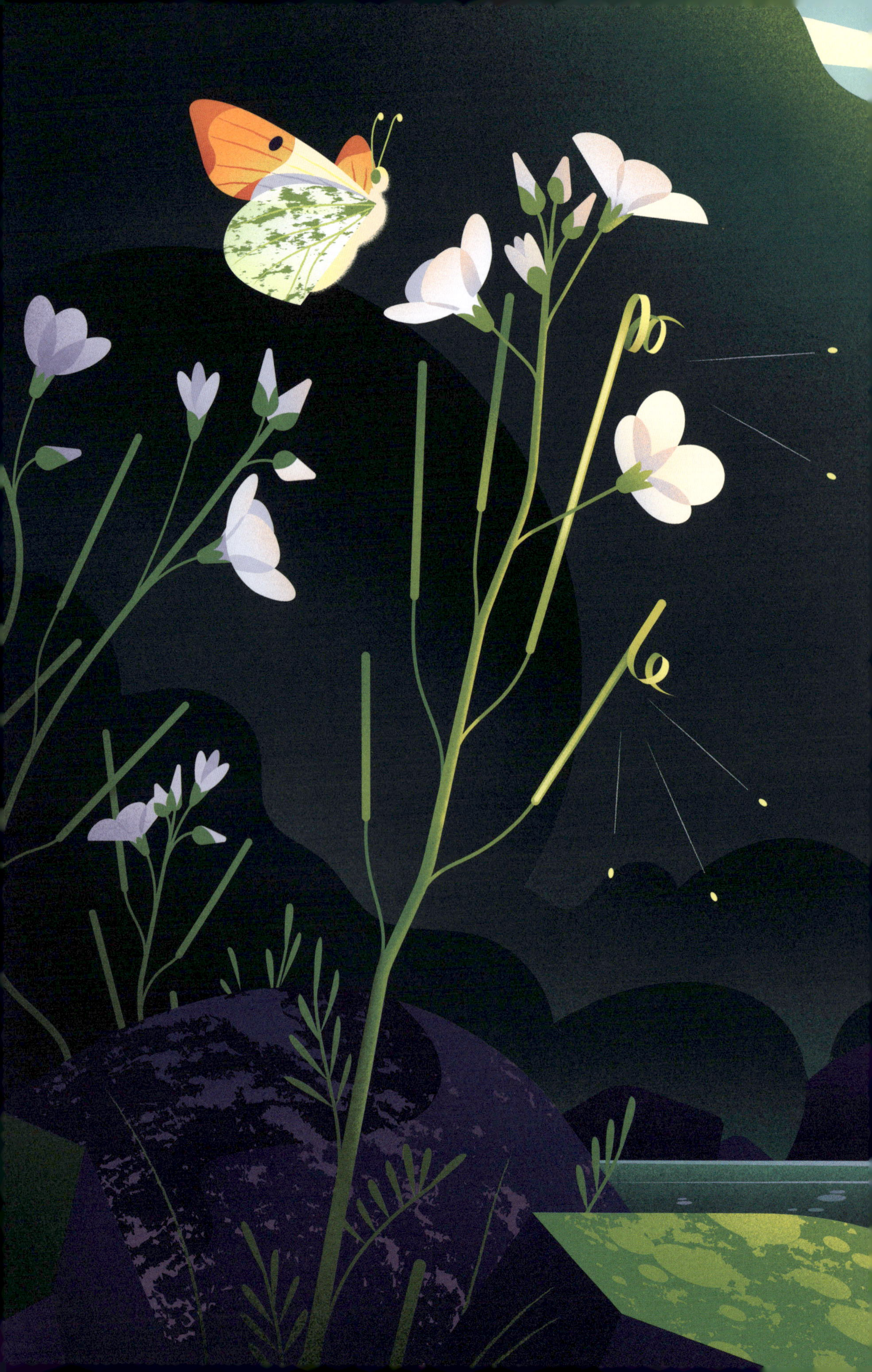

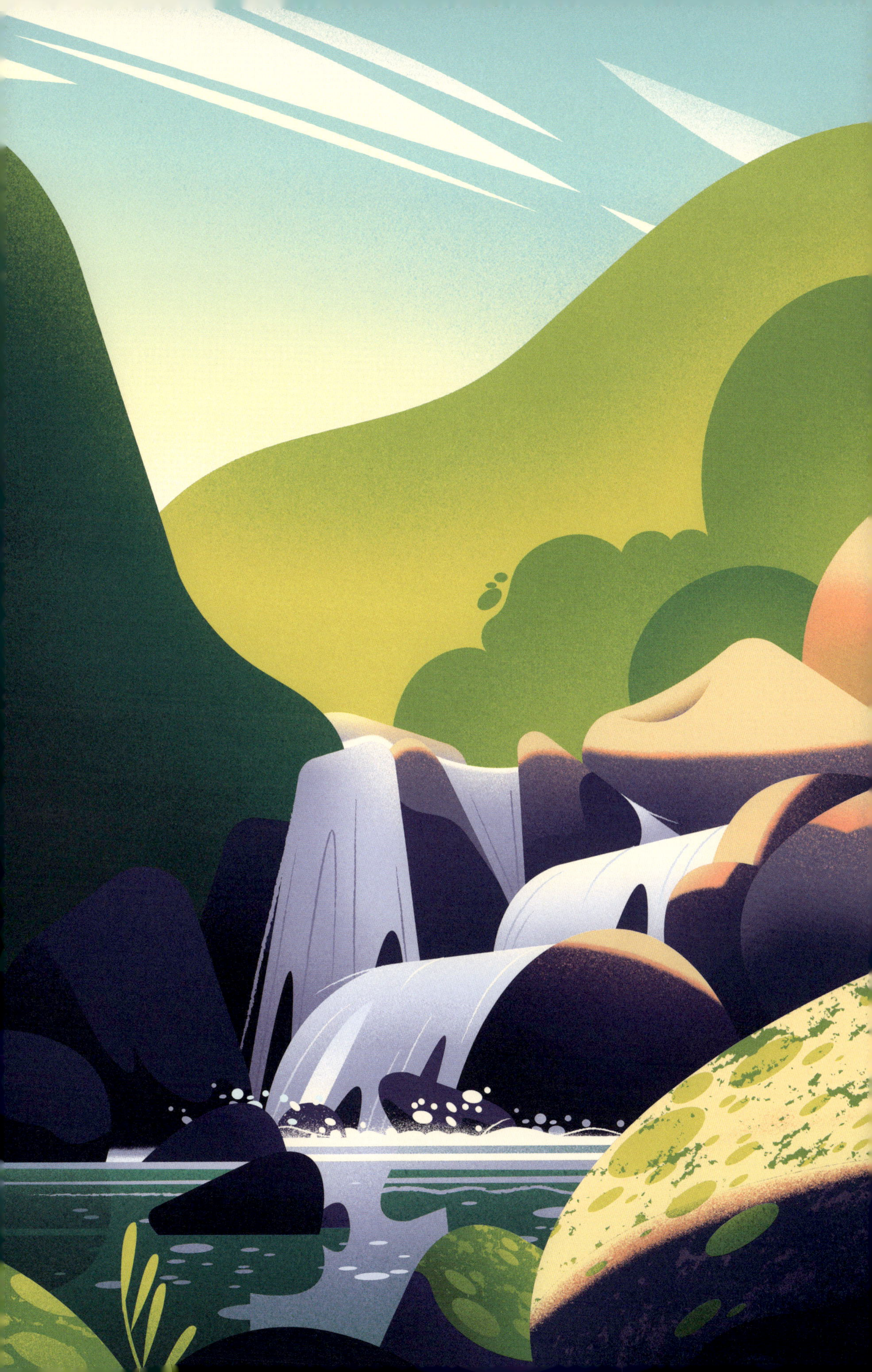

in a flash

Above all, don't be fooled by appearances—some plants have an explosive temperament. Simply brushing against them triggers an onslaught. Boom! In less than a second, their pressurized fruits catapult their seeds far and wide. Preferring to travel alone than in bad company, they rely solely on themselves to disperse.

1. WILD PANSY
Viola tricolor • x 3.5

When the pressure gets too great, the smooth seeds pressed into their capsules make a quick exit.

2. HAIRY BITTERCRESS
Cardamine hirsuta • x 5

At the slightest touch, the capsule contorts and curls up, and projects its tiny seeds into the distance.

3. JAPANESE WISTERIA
Wisteria floribunda • x 1

As it dries, its tough pods slowly contract, then burst open with a sharp bang.

4. SCOTCH BROOM
Cytisus scoparius • x 5

With the heat of summer, the pods suddenly open with an unexpected, joyous crackle.

5. TREE SPURGE
Euphorbia dendroides • x 1.5

Thanks to an explosive release system, this fruit propels its seeds several meters away from the plant.

in a flash

Impatiens noli-tangere

• TOUCH-ME-NOT BALSAM •

hands off!

Lurking in the shadows of a grove, a delicate plant plays at being the princess of the undergrowth. Discreet but impulsive, it reacts to the lightest caress … and that is how it got its name, "touch me not." When ripe, the small, swollen fruits that encapsulate its seeds become extremely sensitive. It's hard to resist tickling them! As soon as you touch them, the valves of the capsule roll up, the fruit explodes, and the seeds slip through your fingers… And the beauty vanishes into the woods!

Geranium robertianum   x 3

113   in a flash

• HERB ROBERT •

victor over asphalt

There is a curious little wild plant that has made itself at home on the sidewalks of our cities. When its flowers make way for thin sword-like fruit, it is time for the assault. Suddenly, the vertically pointed fruit springs up and violently catapults each seed nestling in its cup. Attack! Thanks to this war machine from another time, herb robert conquers every crack in the asphalt! And all under the very noses of passersby...

x 1,5   *Hura crepitans*

• SANDBOX TREE •

terrible crackle

In the rainy season, mysterious crackling sounds can be heard in the Central American rainforests. These are the dry fruits of the sandbox that burst open with a din when they come into contact with water. The valves separating the seeds shatter. With a terrible crackle, the projectiles are sent in all directions. Propelled at a speed of 180 km/h (a record!), they are scattered over a radius of close to 40 meters. Really, it's not a good idea to take shelter under a sandbox tree!

Erodium ciconium x 2

• STORK'S BILL •
astonishing contortionist

Concealed under a tent of tall grass, an astonishing circus act is in the making. Step right up, step right up! Come and see the most beautiful contortionist of them all! With its slender silhouette and corkscrew tail, the stork's bill begins its performance. Depending on the humidity of the air, it twists and turns in all directions. When it is dry, it coils up like a helix; in wet weather, it unfurls and stretches out its entire length. By repeating this spiral movement, the seed gently buries itself as if by magic.

Ecballium elaterium

in a flash

• SQUIRTING CUCUMBER •

confetti cannon

In the heart of a Spanish village, the first summer evenings are tinged with a carefree atmosphere. At this time of year, the fruits of the squirting cucumber, bursting with water, are under pressure. For them, it's time to pop the cork! A slight touch is enough to make them explode. Wham! The fruit detaches itself from the stem and propels dozens of little black seeds into the sky at the remarkable speed of 36 km/h. A fabulous confetti cannon heralding the start of summer!

Punica granatum   x1

• POMEGRANATE •
energy bomb

A real ruby-colored energy bomb, this exquisite fruit delights the taste buds of young and old gourmands alike. Who hasn't enjoyed pomegranate juice? When ripe, its thick skin cracks and bursts open to reveal no fewer than 400 seeds wrapped in a delicious pink pulp. Delivering its scarlet pearls at the drop of a hat, the pomegranate waits for a providential partner to pass by who will possibly disperse its descendants on its travels.

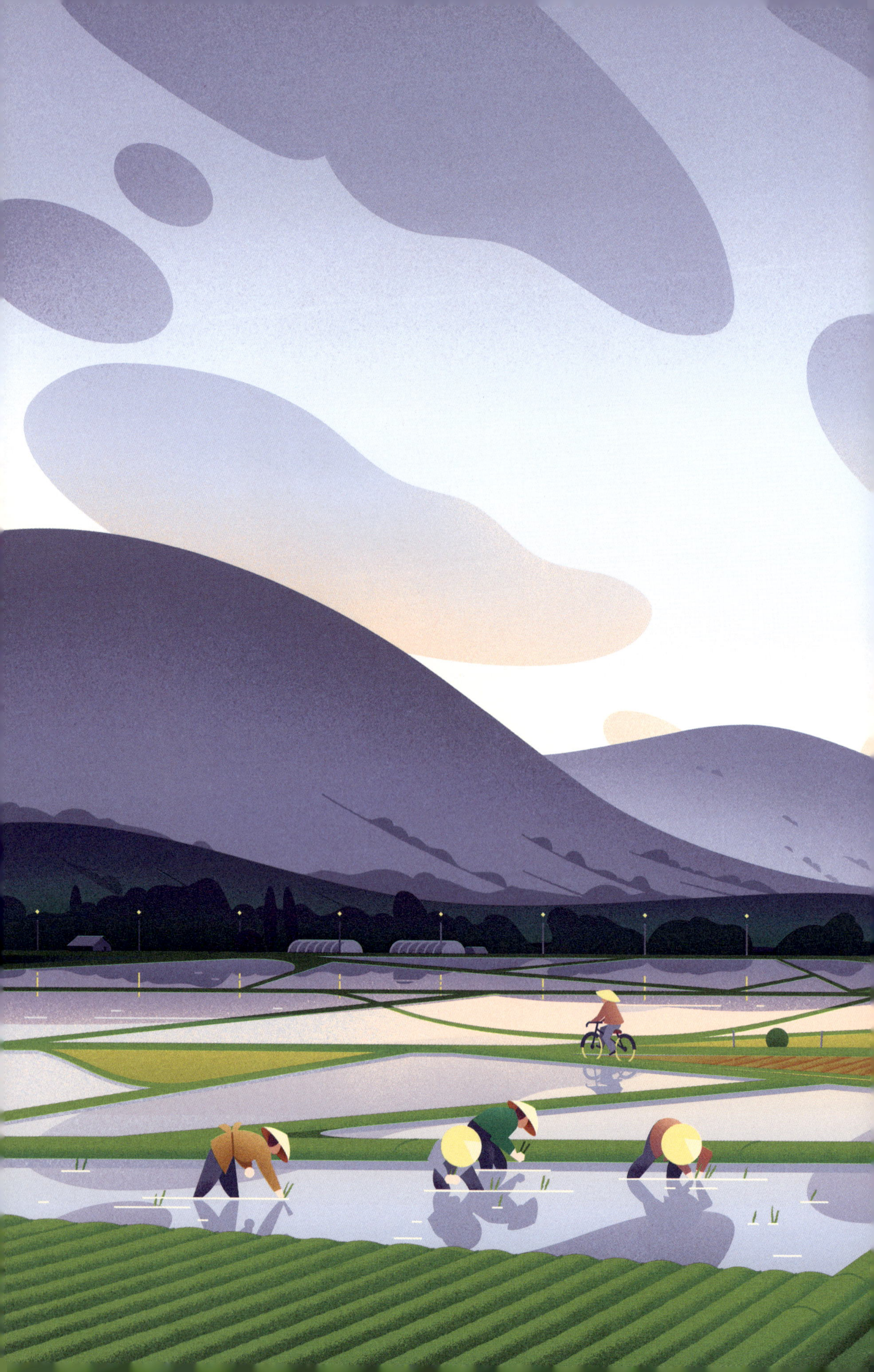

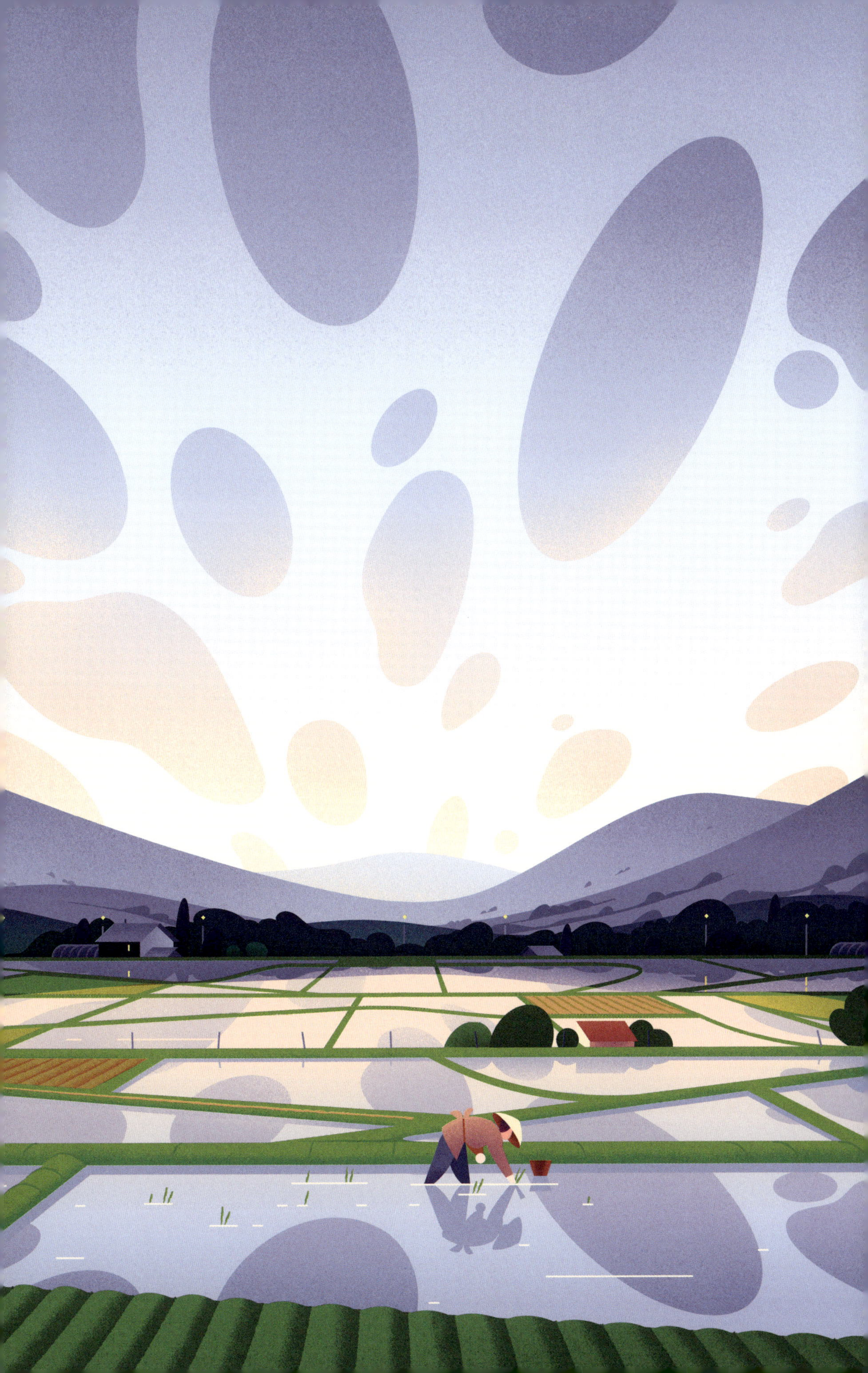

along with humans

Carried in our bags for millennia, these seeds have made their way around the world and played a role in the eventful histories of our civilizations. In turn food, medicine, jewel, or instrument, they have been dispersed by humans through space and time.

1. KOLA NUT
Cola nitida • x 2

The kola nut was one of the basic ingredients in the forerunner ancestor of Coca Cola.

2. ROSARY PEA
Abrus precatorius • x 6,5

Pretty and decorative, this red bead is, nevertheless, terribly poisonous.

3. RUDRAKSHA
Elaeocarpus ganitrus • x 2

These seeds, gathered as a rosary, accompany Buddhist prayer.

4. BLACK PEPPER
Piper nigrum • x 4

The conquistadors of the 15th century sold this spice at the price of gold.

5. FULLER'S TEASEL
Dipsacus sativus • x 1,5

These dried thorny fruits were once used to comb sheep's wool.

6. MAIZE
Zea mays • x 0,5

The Aztecs used these precious golden grains as a currency of exchange.

7. IVORY NUT PALM
Phytelephas macrocarpa • x 1,5

You can carve billiard balls, dice, and combs out of this large seed.

8. WHEAT
Triticum • x 1,5

Cultivated for millennia, wheat feeds a large part of the world's population.

121 along with humans

x 1,5   *Hordeum vulgare*

122 along with humans

· BARLEY ·

in the beginning

About 10,000 years ago, a small group of nomads settled in the hospitable lands of the Fertile Crescent and tried to domesticate the animals and plants around their encampment. This was the beginning of agriculture, and barley was one of the first grains to be cultivated. Over generations, by selecting the seeds, humans transformed this cereal to their liking. The biggest, most resistant grains fed the population and contributed to the growth of many civilizations.

Oryza sativa   x 4

123   along with humans

• RICE •

tiny grain of life

This is the story of a little grain that transformed the landscape of the entire planet. From the high plateaus of the Himalayas to the Mekong Delta, mountains and plains have been shaped by humans to make them suitable for cultivation. Over the millennia, rice paddies have spread across the globe to the extent that, today, rice is the staple food for half of the world's inhabitants. By feeding more than 4 billion people, this tiny grain of life ensures the survival of a large part of humanity.

x 1,5   *Bixa orellana*

• ANNATTO •
new world red

In 1500, Portuguese conquistadors on their way to the Indies landed on the unknown shores of a new world: America. They were greeted by an indigenous people whose skin was entirely covered in a scarlet dye (the origin of the now-offensive epithet "redskins"). This body paint was made from the powerful red pigment of annatto seeds. Its use spread, and today, it is still employed to color smoked fish, cheese, and even lipstick.

Myristica fragrans   x 1,5

· NUTMEG ·

thirst for conquest

In the 16th century, the entire Western world fell for the bewitching fragrance of a spice: nutmeg. Arab merchants, who imported it from the East, did not hesitate to push up the price. Sailors from all over Europe decided to try their luck and set out on expeditions to uncover the secret of its production. When the well-hidden treasure was discovered, the famous nut, living a quiet life on its lush little island in Indonesia, was surprised to find itself involved in a merciless war.

x 2,5

Coffea

along with humans

· COFFEE ·
grain of conviviality

Originating in Ethiopia, coffee has traveled wherever humans have gone. Yemeni monks were the first to appreciate it because it would keep them awake for long stretches of time with clear minds. It then crossed the Mediterranean and met with enormous success at the court of Louis XIV! Coffee houses soon opened across Europe: Paris, London, Vienna... People gathered in these new venues to discuss cultural life and current affairs over a cup of coffee. And that hasn't changed since!

Theobroma cacao   x 0,5

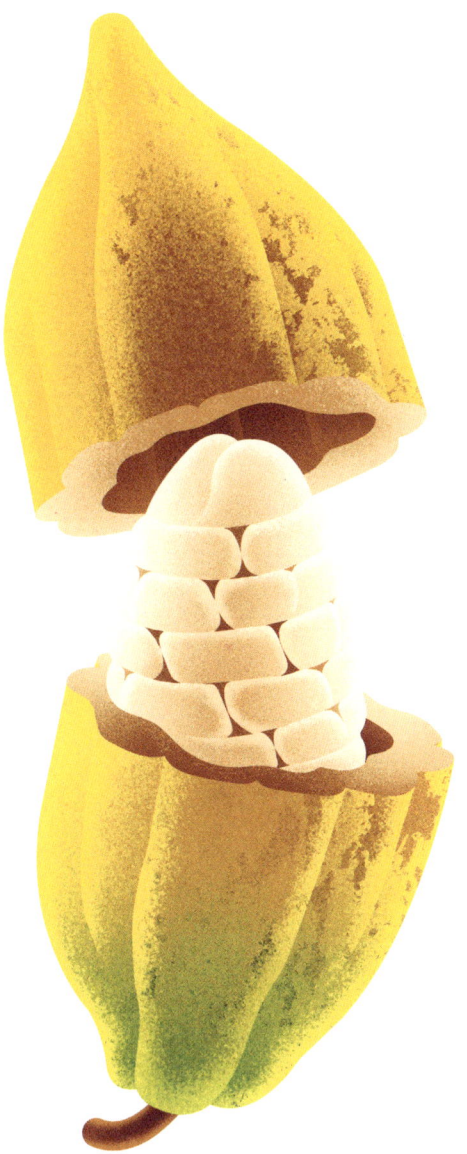

127 along with humans

• CACAO •

sacred bean

Yummy, hot chocolate! This tasty beverage, originally cultivated by the Aztecs, is no longer made to the same ancient recipe. The cocoa beans, roasted and ground, were mixed with water and spices. For many, a real delicacy! The bean was so precious to the Maya that it was used as a currency of exchange: 10 beans were the equivalent of a rabbit, 25 of a terracotta pot. Passing from hand to hand, over time, the bean made its way across the entire continent.

Gossypium

· COTTON ·

a dark history

Who would have imagined that the cultivation of a flower with a delicate pompom could lay at the origin of such a dark chapter in our history? During the industrial revolution, the famous textile fiber that coats the cotton seed contributed to America's growing prosperity. All over the Southern states, cotton plantations flourished, worked by cheap labor: Black slaves transported from Africa by European slave traders. It was to take multiple centuries before slavery was finally abolished.

Papaver somniferum   x 3,5

129   along with humans

• OPIUM POPPY •

opium madness

The poppy has long been appreciated for its therapeutic virtues. It's a true medicinal plant. However, its history took an unexpected turn in the 19th century. A powerful soporific became widespread in the English suburbs. Opium, derived from the pods of this variety of poppy, produced a hypnotic effect whose merits were extolled by the thinkers and artists of the time. But the accursed substance is also devastatingly addictive, and this medicine soon became a drug with disastrous consequences.

x 5,5

Ricinus communis

130 along with humans

• CASTOR OIL PLANT •

deadly poison

Don't let appearances fool you. The pretty castor bean contains one of world's most toxic poisons, worse than cyanide or arsenic! A few drops of ricin are enough to kill a person! And KGB agents knew this all too well. During the Cold War, some spies used it to wipe out opponents of the Communist regime who they felt were too free with their opinion, or else had loose lips. The victim, seized by fever and terrible fits of vomiting, often succumbed before the assassin could be found.

Ceratonia siliqua   x 1,5

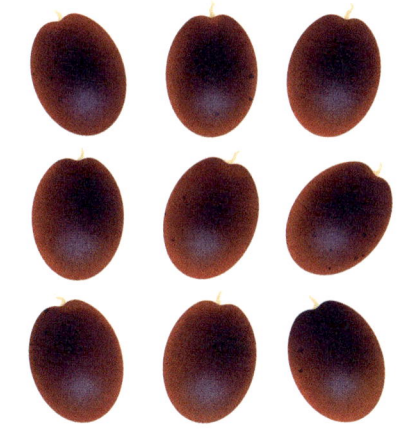

• CAROB •

precious weight

What do diamonds and carob seeds have in common? The carat! In ancient times, these seeds were used by Egyptian, Greek, and Roman merchants returning from expeditions. These little brown beads always have the same weight and were used as a measure in the gold and gemstone trade: 1 gram corresponds to 5 carats, or 5 carob seeds. In 1905, an enormous diamond was extracted from the depths of a mine near Pretoria: it weighed 620 grams or 3,100 carats!

x 0,5

Lagenaria siceraria

· CALABASH ·

generous by nature

Long before the invention of pottery, the calabash served as a vessel used by people on every continent and across many cultures. Its striking shape was not without its assets. For Massai shepherds, it was a flask, for others, a bowl, a salver, a spoon, or even a musical instrument. The first maracas were simply dried gourds with their seeds trapped inside. Musicians would keep the beat by shaking them ... Nature is definitely generous to those who know how to use their imagination!

133 along with humans

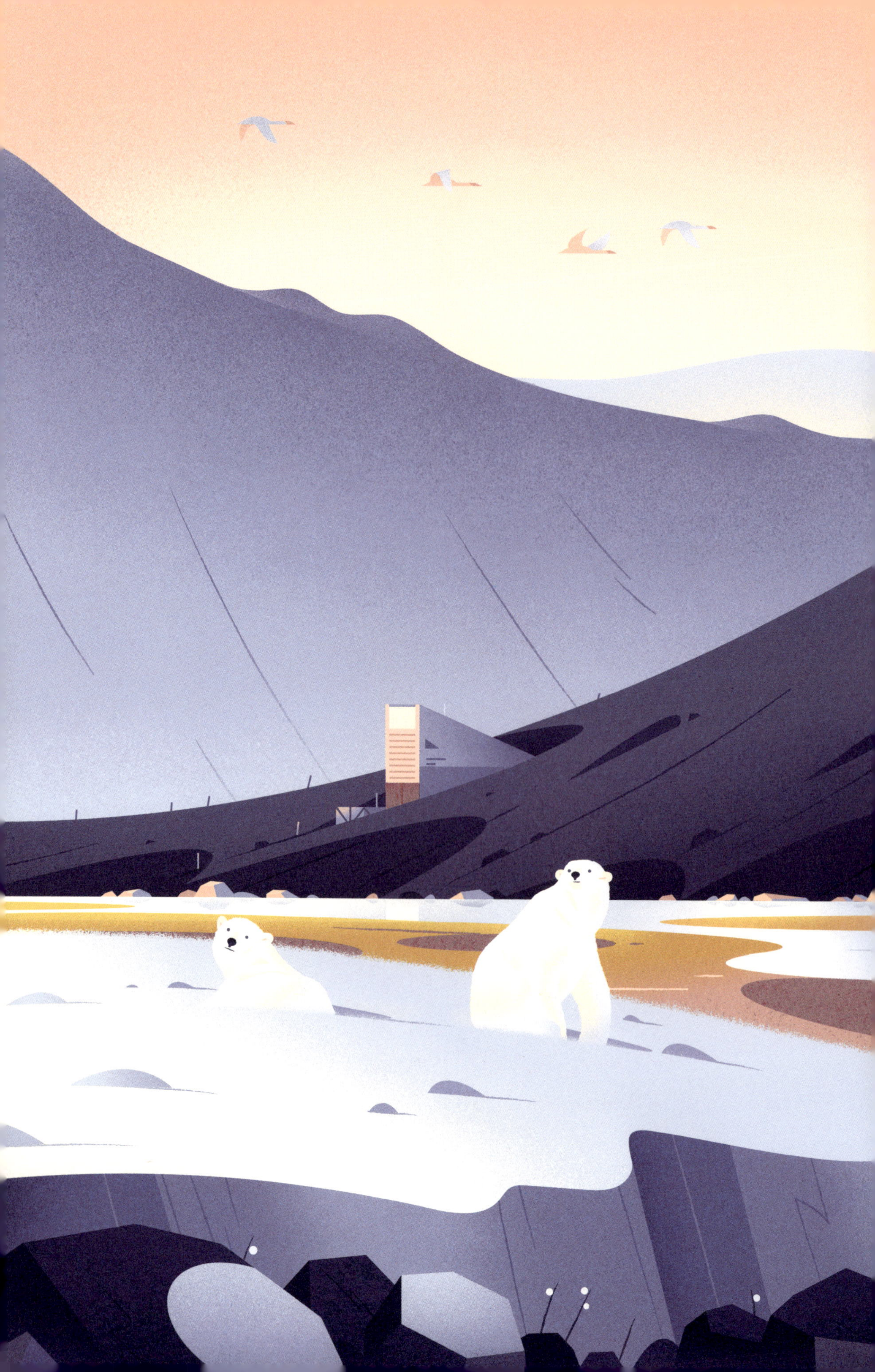

Nothing seems to grow in the frozen lands of the Arctic. However, buried in the depths, an extraordinary place shelters precious life in slumber. This is the Svalbard Global Seed Vault, one of the largest on Earth. More than a million seeds, collected from the four corners of the world, are stored in this vault: a real treasure trove for preserving biodiversity and the future of humanity. Seeds are an essential resource for all beings on our planet! By taking care of them and the environment, humankind helps to maintain a rich and fertile ecosystem.

Our future depends on it. It's up to each of us to exert ourselves on behalf of all life!

some shortcuts

travel...

For hundreds of millions of years, plants have worked out ingenious stratagems to enable their seeds to liberate themselves and disperse. Long- or short-distance traveler, each sets out on its own odyssey.

with just a puff of air

Light and tiny, these seeds are bona fide conquistadors. The air is their ally: a simple puff carries them off to new countries.
—
Artichoke • Clematis • Plane Tree • St. John's Wort • Star Clover • White Campion • Dandelion • Shepherd's Purse • Button Burclover • Scabious • Birthwort • Greater Quaking Grass • Field Poppy • Foxglove

on the wind

The biggest seeds must compete in ingenuity to keep suspended or else propel themselves: wings, capes, gliders, rolling carriages, or flying capsules…
—
African Tulip Tree • Heart Pea • European Hornbeam • Hora • Ash • Hop Tree • Bush Willow • Sugar Maple • Javan Cucumber • Feather Grass • Honesty • Linden • Wild Carrot • Bladder Senna • Japanese Lantern • Tumbleweed

on the water

From the runoff caused by storms to the great currents that govern our oceans, water carries certain seeds to distant regions.

—

Mary's Bean • Water Caltrop • Sea Daffodil • White Water Lily • Gray Nicker • Yellow Water Lily • Horse Eye Bean • Coconut • Red Mangrove • Sacred Lotus • Fish Poison Tree • Sea Bean • Water Chestnut • Flag Iris

---

all fired up

Summer heat waves and fires are the worst enemies of most plants. But extreme heat is synonymous with tactical flight for some.

—

Woody Pear • Spruce • Mountain Devil • Rose Banksia • Rock Rose • Atlas Cedar • Giant Sequoia • Aleppo Pine • Black Spruce • Firewood Banksia • Ironwood • Blue Gum • Silver Tree • Crimson Bottlebrush

---

small steps, big deal

Some seeds have signed a pact with ants. In exchange for transportation, the plants offer them tasty treats.

—

Bleeding Heart • Large Mediterranean Spurge • Snowdrop • Hairy Woodrush • Bloodroot • Bear's Foot • Greater Celandine • Cornflower • Sweet Violet • Boxwood • Coastal Wattle

winging it
68

Some seeds are surprisingly mischievous. Before setting out on their epic journey, they recruit feathered friends.
—
Italian arum • Dog Rose • Elderberry • Bird of Paradise • Swiss Pine • Peony • Spindle Tree • Water Liana • Doussie • Yew • Redoul • Mistletoe • Five-Horned Spindle • Traveler's Tree • Blueberry • Guarana • Bastard Hogberry

on all fours
82

Clinging to a sheep's fleece or nestling in a mouse's stomach, some seeds play stowaway and roam about at the whim of their ride.
—
Tickseed • Cleaver • Sticklewort • Sour Cherry • Marigold • Hazelnut • Devil's Claw • Magnolia • Elephant's Ear • Ram's Horn • Wild Oat • Canadian Tick-Trefoil • African Baobab • Oak • Wild Strawberry • Lantern Tree • Devil's Thorn • Burdock

in free fall
98

Not very daring, these seeds do not have the stuff of great adventurers. Taking advantage of the law of gravity, they simply let themselves fall and roll along the ground.
—
Inca Peanut • Garden Pea • Lentil • Horse Chestnut • Chickpea • Black Hickory • Cannonball Tree • Chestnut • English Walnut • Coco de Mer • Avocado • Brazil Nut

in a flash

In less than a second, some pressurized fruits catapult their seeds far and wide. They rely solely on themselves to disperse.

—

Wild Pansy • Hairy Bittercress • Japanese Wisteria • Scotch Broom • Tree Spurge • Touch-Me-Not Balsam • Herb Robert • Sandbox Tree • Stork's Bill • Squirting Cucumber • Pomegranate

---

along with humans

Carried in our bags for millennia, these seeds have made their way around the world and played a role in the eventful histories of our civilizations.

—

Kola Nut • Rosary Pea • Rudraksha • Black Pepper • Fuller's Teasel • Maize • Ivory Nut Palm • Wheat • Barley • Rice • Annatto • Nutmeg • Coffee • Cacao • Cotton • Opium Poppy • Castor Oil Plant • Carob • Calabash

... in a few figures

200 °C

The temperature necessary for the ironwood to open the scales of its cones and set its little winged seeds free. A real inferno!

A real inferno!

p. 53

the most toxic

6,000 times more poisonous than cyanide and 12,000 times more dangerous than a rattlesnake's venom, nothing equals the toxicity of ricin.

p. 130

p. 127

The Maya used the cacao bean as a precious currency of exchange.

10 beans = 1 rabbit

36 km/h

With the great speed at which it expels its seeds, the squirting cucumber sets a real record!

p. 116

20,000 km

The sea bean can travel halfway around the globe surfing on the Gulf Stream.

pp. 40–41

95 million years

The ancestor of the magnolia appeared in the age of the dinosaurs.

p. 86

130 millimeters

The Javan cucumber produces one of the largest winged seeds.

p. 23

4 billion people

Rice nourishes more than half of the world's inhabitants.

p. 123

25 million metric tons/year

Cotton is the world's most widely produced natural fiber.

p. 128

2 meters

The giant pod of the sea bean can be larger than a human: a real champion!

pp. 40-41

3 milliseconds

The pod of the hairy bittercress explodes at an incredible speed.

p. 111

10,000 years

Barley was one of the first grains cultivated by humans.

p. 122

20 kg

The coco de mer takes the top place on the podium in the heavyweight category!

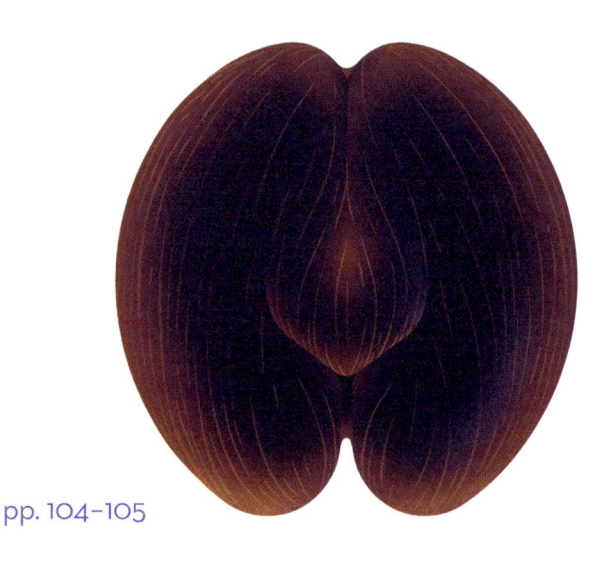

pp. 104-105

Powerful psychotropic

In equal proportions, the guarana contains at least 4 times as much caffeine as Arabica coffee. If you're hyperactive, abstain!

p. 80

400,000 seeds/year

Sequoias top the list of the most productive trees!

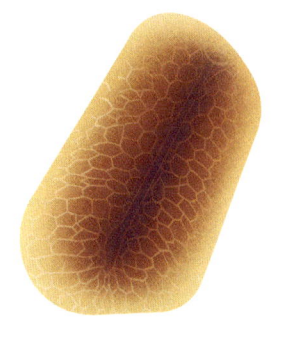

p. 49

p. 17

0.00001 g

The foxglove produces the smallest seeds in Europe. It takes 10,000 to make up 1 gram!

1,300 Years

The sacred lotus holds a record for longevity!

p. 38

145

...from one letter to the next

a

AFRICAN BAOBAB	*Adansonia digitata*	92
AFRICAN TULIP TREE	*Spathodea campanulata*	20
ALEPPO PINE	*Pinus halepensis*	50
ANNATTO	*Bixa orellana*	124
ASH	*Fraxinus sp.*	20–21
ARTICHOKE	*Cynara cardunculus*	8–9
ATLAS CEDAR	*Cedrus atlantica*	48
AVOCADO	*Persea americana*	106

b

BARLEY	*Hordeum vulgare*	122, 144
BASTARD HOGBERRY	*Margaritaria nobilis*	81
BEAR'S FOOT	*Helleborus foetidus*	62
BIRD OF PARADISE	*Strelitzia reginae*	70–71
BIRTHWORT	*Aristolochia elegans*	14
BLACK HICKORY	*Carya texana*	100–101
BLACK PEPPER	*Piper nigrum*	120–121
BLACK SPRUCE	*Picea mariana*	51
BLADDER SENNA	*Colutea arborescens*	29
BLEEDING HEART	*Dicentra sp.*	60–61
BLOODROOT	*Sanguinaria canadensis*	60–61
BLUE GUM	*Eucalyptus globulus*	54
BLUEBERRY	*Vaccinium myrtillus*	79
BOXWOOD	*Buxus sempervirens*	66
BRAZIL NUT	*Bertholletia excelsa*	107
BURDOCK	*Arctium*	97
BUSH WILLOW	*Combretum*	20–21
BUTTON BURCLOVER	*Medicago orbicularis*	12

c

CACAO	*Theobroma cacao*	127, 142
CALABASH	*Lagenaria siceraria*	132–133
CANADIAN TICK-TREFOIL	*Desmodium canadense*	91
CANNONBALL TREE	*Couroupita guianensis*	100–101
CAROB	*Ceratonia siliqua*	131
CASTOR OIL PLANT	*Ricinus communis*	130
CHESTNUT	*Castanea*	102
CHICKPEA	*Cicer arietinum*	100–101
CLEAVER	*Galium aparine*	84–85
CLEMATIS	*Clematis flammula*	8–9
COASTAL WATTLE	*Acacia cyclops*	67
COCO DE MER	*Lodoicea maldivica*	104–105, 144

	COCONUT	*Cocos nucifera*	36
	COFFEE	*Coffea*	126
	CORNFLOWER	*Centaurea cyanus*	64
	COTTON	*Gossypium*	128, 143
	CRIMSON BOTTLEBRUSH	*Callistemon citrinus*	56
d	DANDELION	*Leontodon taraxacum*	10
	DEVIL'S CLAW	*Harpagophytum procumbens*	84–85
	DEVIL'S THORN	*Tribulus terrestris*	96
	DOG ROSE	*Rosa canina*	70–71
	DOUSSI	*Afzelia Africana*	72–73
e	ELDERBERRY	*Sambucus*	70–71
	ELEPHANT'S EAR	*Enterolobium cyclocarpum*	86
	ENGLISH WALNUT	*Juglans regia*	103
	EUROPEAN HORNBEAM	*Carpinus betulus*	20–21
f	FEATHER GRASS	*Stipa pennata*	25
	FIELD POPPY	*Papaver rhoeas*	16
	FIREWOOD BANKSIA	*Banksia menziesii*	52
	FISH POISON TREE	*Barringtonia asiatica*	39
	FIVE-HORNED SPINDLE	*Euonymus cornutus*	75
	FLAG IRIS	*Iris pseudacorus*	43
	FOXGLOVE	*Digitalis purpurea*	17, 145
	FULLER'S TEASEL	*Dipsacus sativus*	120–121
g	GARDEN PEA	*Pisum sativum*	100–101
	GIANT SEQUOIA	*Sequoiadendron giganteum*	49, 145
	GRAY NICKER	*Caesalpinia bonduc*	34–35
	GREATER CELANDINE	*Chelidonium majus*	63
	GREATER QUAKING GRASS	*Briza maxima*	15
	GUARANA	*Paullinia cupana*	80, 145
h	HAIRY BITTERCRESS	*Cardamine hirsuta*	110–111, 144
	HAIRY WOODRUSH	*Luzula Pilosa*	60–61
	HAZELNUT	*Corylus avellana*	84–85
	HEART PEA	*Cardiospermum halicacabum*	20–21
	HERB ROBERT	*Geranium robertianum*	113
	HONESTY	*Lunaria*	26
	HOP TREE	*Ptelea trifoliata*	20–21
	HORA	*Dipterocarpus zeylanicus*	20–21
	HORSE CHESTNUT	*Aesculus hippocastanum*	100–101
	HORSE EYE BEAN	*Mucuna sloanei*	34–35
i	INCA PEANUT	*Plukenetia volubilis*	100–101
	IRONWOOD	*Casuarina collina*	53, 142
	ITALIAN ARUM	*Arum italicum*	70–71
	IVORY NUT PALM	*Phytelephas macrocarpa*	120–121

j
JAPANESE LANTERN	*Physalis*	30
JAPANESE WISTERIA	*Wisteria floribunda*	110–111
JAVAN CUCUMBER	*Alsomitra macrocarpa*	23, 143

k
KOLA NUT	*Cola nitida*	120–121

l
LANTERN TREE	*Hernandia nymphaeifolia*	95
LARGE MEDITERRANEAN SPURGE	*Euphorbia characias*	60–61
LENTIL	*Lens culinaris*	100–101
LINDEN	*Tilia*	27

m
MAGNOLIA	*Magnolia*	86, 143
MAIZE CORN	*Zea mays*	120–121
MARIGOLD	*Calendula*	84–85
MARY'S BEAN	*Merremia discoidesperma*	34–35
MISTLETOE	*Viscum album*	76
MOUNTAIN DEVIL	*Lambertia Formosa*	46–47

n
NUTMEG	*Myristica fragrans*	125

o
OAK	*Quercus ilex*	93
OPIUM POPPY	*Papaver somniferum*	129

p
PEONY	*Paeonia*	70–71
PLANE TREE	*Platanus acerifolia*	8–9
POMEGRANATE	*Punica granatum*	117

r
RAM'S HORN	*Proboscidea louisianica*	88–89
RED MANGROVE	*Rhizophora mangle*	37
REDOUL	*Coriaria myrtifolia*	75
RICE	*Oryza sativa*	123, 143
ROCK ROSE	*Cistus*	46–47
ROSARY PEA	*Abrus precatorius*	120–121
ROSE BANKSIA	*Banksia laricina*	46–47
RUDRAKSHA	*Elaeocarpus ganitrus*	120–121

s
SACRED LOTUS	*Nelumbo nucifera*	38, 145
ST. JOHN'S WORT	*Hypericum sp.*	8–9
SANDBOX TREE	*Hura crepitans*	114
SCABIOUS	*Scabiosa*	13
SCOTCH BROOM	*Cytisus scoparius*	110–111
SEA BEAN	*Entada gigas*	40–41, 143, 144
SEA DAFFODIL	*Pancratium maritimum*	34–35
SHEPHERD'S PURSE	*Capsella bursa-pastoris*	11

	SILVER TREE	*Leucadendron argenteum*	55
	SNOWDROP	*Galanthus nivalis*	60–61
	SOUR CHERRY	*Prunus cerasus*	84–85
	SPINDLE TREE	*Euonymus*	70–71
	SPRUCE	*Picea abies*	46–47
	SQUIRTING CUCUMBER	*Ecballium elaterium*	116, 142
	STAR CLOVER	*Trifolium stellatum*	8–9
	STICKLEWORT	*Agrimonia eupatoria*	84–85
	STORK'S BILL	*Erodium ciconium*	115
	SUGAR MAPLE	*Acer saccharum*	22
	SWEET VIOLET	*Viola odorata*	65
	SWISS PINE	*Pinus cembra*	70–71
t	TICKSEED	*Bidens sp*	84–85
	TOUCH-ME-NOT BALSAM	*Impatiens noli-tangere*	112
	TRAVELER'S TREE	*Ravenala madagascariensis*	76
	TREE SPURGE	*Euphorbia dendroides*	110–111
	TUMBLEWEED	*Salsola tragus*	31
w	WATER CALTROP	*Trapa natans*	34–35
	WATER CHESTNUT	*Trapa bicornis*	42
	WATER LIANA	*Tetracera billardierei*	70–71
	WHEAT	*Triticum*	120–121
	WHITE CAMPION	*Silene latifolia*	8–9
	WHITE WATER LILY	*Nymphaea alba*	34–35
	WILD CARROT	*Daucus carota*	28
	WILD OAT	*Avena fatua*	90
	WILD PANSY	*Viola tricolor*	110–111
	WILD STRAWBERRY	*Fragaria vesca*	94
	WOODY PEAR	*Xylomelum angustifolium*	46–47
y	YELLOW WATER LILY	*Nuphar lutea*	34–35
	YEW	*Taxus*	74

I grew up at the foot of the Cévennes mountains in France. Oaks, cedars, and chestnut trees are the arcades of my cathedral. I love to recharge my batteries among this family of silent giants, to caress their bark, harvest their seeds, smell the earth, and find a welcoming place to extend my roots alongside them. Scotch pine, spruce, larch, eucalyptus ... the fibers of all of these magnificent trees were used to make the paper pulp needed to produce this book. I offer them my thanks and, for that reason, this book is dedicated to them.

The idea behind this book is my desire to share my wonder at nature's ingenuity with a wide readership. Those who are well-versed in botany will note that sometimes the word "seed" refers to the "children" of plants: this is to say, both the seed and the fruit. I decided to do this because, in popular imagery, seeds and fruits are linked with each other. I chose to illustrate them here in all their diversity and break away from scientific vocabulary with the intention of offering my sensitive, poetic perspective to as many people as possible. May the specialists forgive this artistic license!

This book benefited greatly from the scientific contribution of Yves Pauthier, head of the seed bank at the Muséum national d'histoire naturelle, the national museum of natural history in Paris.

On the course of my long journey, I have been fortunate to encounter the work of sentinels who—with a sharp eye—have scrutinized the beauty of the plant world to understand it better: photographers, illustrators, botanists, ecologists, writers, historians, philosophers, filmmakers... All are united by the same burning passion of being able to share their valuable knowledge with us. In the following list, I provide you with some of the works that have marked my pilgrimage: Karl Blossfeldt, *The Complete Published Work*, Cologne, 2014 • Levon Biss, *The Hidden Beauty of Seeds & Fruits*, New York, 2021 • Michel Butor and Paul Starosta, *Graines*, Milan, 2016 • Katie Scott and Kathy Willis, *Botanicum*, London, 2017 • José Ramón Alonso and Marco Paschetta, *Semillas. Un pequeño gran viaje*, Barcelona, 2018 • Francis Hallé, *Atlas of Poetic Botany*, Cambridge (MA), 2018 • Estelle Zhong Mengual, *Apprendre à voir. Le point de vue du vivant*, Arles, 2021 • Thor Hanson, *The Triumph of Seeds*, New York, 2015 • Renato Bruni, *Erba volant*, Turin, 2015 • Jean-Marie Pelt, *La vie sociale des plantes*, Vanves, 2019 • Peter Wohlleben, *The Hidden Life of Trees*, Vancouver, 2016 • Emmanuelle Grundmann, Noémie Levain, and Muriel Hazan, *Graines et fruits*, Arles, 2012 • Benoît Garrone, Philippe Martin, and Bertrand Schatz, *Stratégies végétales*, Prades-le-Lez, 2011 • Serge Schall, *Graines*, Toulouse, 2020 • *La vie partout. 10 minutes pour comprendre le vivant*, podcast by Quentin Travaillé, 2022 • *La vie secrète des plantes*, documentary series in three episodes by Son Seung-woo, broadcast on Arte, 2019 • David Attenborough's *The Green Planet*, documentary series in five episodes directed by Paul Williams, Peter Bassett, Rosie Thomas, and Elisabeth Oakham, broadcast on the BBC, 2022.

My very special thanks go to Simon, who accompanies me daily on my crazy odysseys. He is my first reader and major safeguard. To Véronique, for her attentive listening, patience, and meticulous involvement in the writing and publication of this work. This book would not exist without her. To Colline, Director of Giboulées, for her ceaseless support, her enthusiasm, and unshakeable trust. The team at Giboulées, the Gallimard publishing house, and all the people who have contributed in any way to making this project possible. As well as to all the people in the world of books who work every day to pass on knowledge, and who—by taking part in this adventure—will make small seeds germinate in all of our spirits. Here's wishing this book a long life!

Manufacturing a book is far from being without consequences for the environment. While creating this book, I was determined to reconcile aesthetic demands with environmental commitment. This desire conditioned certain artistic choices: paper, inks, printing processes… I tried to instill this conviction in the editorial team assisting me. Together, we worked toward this goal. Although it is not easy to change the world, it is always possible to get things moving.
Sometimes, a little can go a long way!

Seeds was printed by Lego, in Vicenza, at the foot of the Italian Alps, on Arena Natural Smooth 140g paper in the fall of 2024 during chestnut and acorn season. The cover of this edition is an exclusive creation by Cruschiform, designed for the English and German editions of the book.

© for the French edition: 2024 Gallimard Jeunesse
for illustrations, texts, conception and realization: 2024 Cruschiform
© for the English edition: 2024, Prestel Verlag, Munich · London · New York
A member of Penguin Random House Verlagsgruppe GmbH
Neumarkter Strasse 28 · 81673 Munich

The publisher expressly reserves the right to exploit the copyrighted content of this work for the purposes of text and data mining in accordance with Section 44b of the German Copyright Act (UrhG), based on the European Digital Single Market Directive. Any unauthorized use is an infringement of copyright and is hereby prohibited.

Library of Congress Control Number: 2024945502
A CIP catalogue record for this book is available from the British Library.

Translated from French by Robert McInnes
Project Management: Constanze Holler
Copyediting: José Enrique Macián
Production Management: Susanne Hermann
Typesetting: satz-bau Leingärtner, Nabburg
Printing and Binding: L.E.G.O., Vicenza

Penguin Random House Verlagsgruppe FSC® N001967

Printed in Italy

ISBN 978-3-7913-7596-0

www.prestel.com

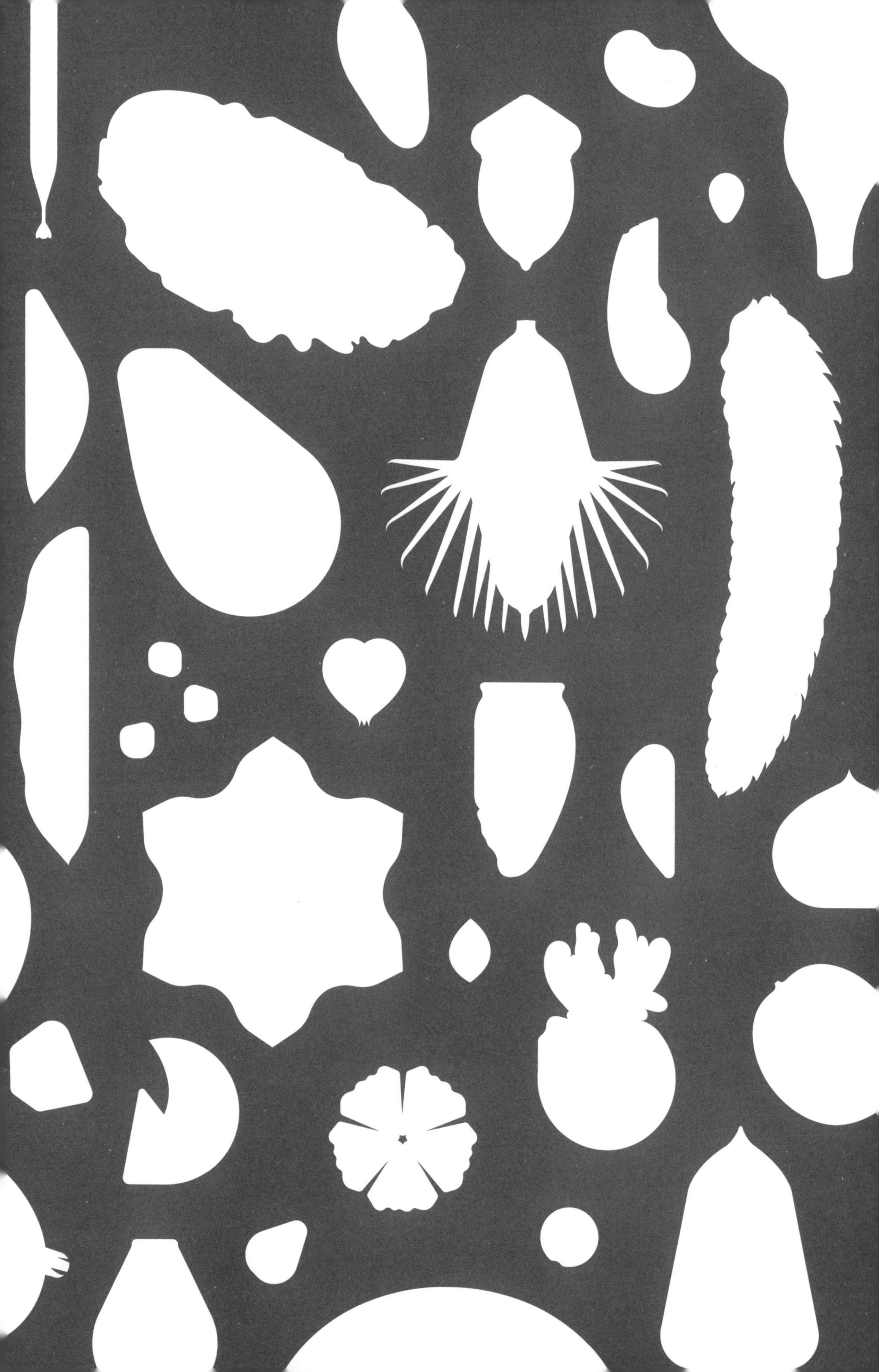